11/11/81

→ The Art of

ISAAC BABEL

by PATRICIA CARDEN

Cornell University Press

ITHACA AND LONDON

First published 1972 by Cornell University Press.
Published in the United Kingdom by Cornell University Press Ltd.,
2–4 Brook Street, London W1Y 1AA.

International Standard Book Number 0-8014-0720-6
Library of Congress Catalog Card Number 72–2359
PRINTED IN THE UNITED STATES OF AMERICA
BY VAIL-BALLOU PRESS, INC.

Librarians: Library of Congress cataloging information
appears on the last page of the book.

For my parents

Contents

Preface

In his life Isaac Babel published three cycles of stories:
the Odessa stories, which deal comically with a group of
Jewish gangsters; the *Red Cavalry* stories, which are based
on his own experiences with Budenny's First Cavalry during its campaign against the Whites in the Ukraine and
eastern Poland in 1920; and the stories of childhood, which
are based on Babel's own youth in Odessa and in a little
town on the coast of the Black Sea. Besides these three
cycles, which constitute the greater part of his work, he
wrote two plays and a few other stories. The whole work
is contained in a neat little volume that fits easily into the
hand.

The stories upon which Babel's fame rests are very short.
He never published a story that was more than ten pages
long, and most of his stories run about six pages. In answer
to a heckler who wanted to know why he did not write
long novels in the manner of Tolstoy, Babel once quoted
Goethe's "definition" of the novella: "a very short story,
that genre in which I feel more comfortable than in any
other." Babel appropriated the genre of the novella for his
own and became its master. It would be difficult to name a
writer who has surpassed Babel in his chosen form.

One of the mysteries connected with Babel (and he is a man of mystery, a real Sebastian Knight awaiting his Nabokov) concerns the sizable reputation that his very slight body of work has acquired. Another mystery has to do with the interpretation of the works themselves. Short as the stories are, they suggest a very complex and paradoxical view of the world. Yet this view is somehow hidden and difficult to define. "Just what does Babel mean to say to us? What is his real attitude toward the world?" It is difficult to write about Babel without adopting this tone.

Art was for Babel the most serious thing in life, the cruel master which he served and to which he sacrificed. Indeed, Babel was one of the modern priests of art for whom art conferred meaning on life. He would rather have been called artist than any other title. Happily, the title is one that he richly deserves.

I chose to study Babel because I was moved by the excellence of the stories. He so clearly deserves the kind of attention we accord to great writers. I was moved, too, by the enigmatic quality of the work, intrigued by Babel's game. A philosopher said to me, "You must not be afraid to say that Babel is profound." Babel satisfies the inner eye seeking the comfort of pattern, but he satisfies the mind as well. His is the art of the mind's imagination, transforming the evidence of the senses into meaning.

The proximity of Babel's compact stories to poetry has often been observed. I have tried to do justice to their density of meaning and design by the kind of close reading we have come to take for granted in the study of poetry. My own first literary interest was English poetry of the seventeenth and twentieth centuries. Babel's stories, I found, fit into this context easily. This surprising intuition has been my point of departure. The poetry of these periods has suggested the avenues of approach to Babel's hyperbolic, intellectual, metaphysical prose.

I have tried to balance the claims of the individual stories against the claims of the cycles and of the work as a whole. The stories inevitably lose when we use them to draw the shape of the cycle. To make up for this loss, I have tried to convey, through full readings of a number of stories, their individual depth and richness. At the same time I have sketched out the fuller view of Babel's work as a whole that I have come to through a close reading of the stories.

Babel's life has stood like a shadow between the reader and the stories for many years. As a Jew and as a victim of Stalin's purges, he has evoked an easy interest, often at the expense of the stories themselves. Babel was impatient with his life when it interfered with his art, and he would be impatient with his readers for their lack of discernment. I hope to right the balance, to focus attention where it belongs. We can feel only humility before the extraordinary rigors Babel subjected himself to as artist. To read Babel with comparable rigor is my goal.

The study has been read in earlier stages by a number of people who made helpful suggestions for its improvement, among them Alexander Erlich, George Gibian, William E. Harkins, Richard F. Kuhns, Robert Maguire, Nathan Rosen, and Lionel Trilling. I am particularly indebted to Martin Horwitz, who took a lively and beneficial interest in the work during the entire course of its development. Most important of all have been the continuing kind interest and wise counsel of Rufus W. Mathewson, Jr.

Grants from the Ford Foundation and the Inter-University Committee on Travel Grants supported my research. Patricia Blake was generous in sharing the fruits of her research on Babel, and Nathalie Babel has been more than generous in allowing me to see the materials she has collected before they were prepared for publication.

PATRICIA CARDEN

Ithaca, New York

A Note on Transliteration

The system of transliteration for Russian words and names used in the text is System II from *The Transliteration of Modern Russian for English-Language Publications* by J. Thomas Shaw (Madison: University of Wisconsin Press, 1967). This is the Library of Congress system for transliteration of modern Russian with the diacritical marks omitted.

The Art of
ISAAC BABEL

1. Frontispiece:
A Sketch of the Writer

"Among the various forms of depersonalization we must include the depersonalization of a writer's biography." Babel's joke has the sad ring of truth when we look at his "biography." The picture of the writer that emerges from the reminiscences and letters that have appeared in recent years shares the masklike quality of the heroes of his stories.[1] Nor is Babel's own account of his life very helpful. He applied his mythmaking powers even to his autobiography, offering now one, now another version of his life as it suited the political convenience of the moment.[2]

[1] The most adequate biography of Babel to appear thus far is Part I of *Isaac Babel', 1894–1941: L'homme et l'oeuvre* by Judith Stora-Sandor. A useful chronology of Babel's life and work, compiled from all the known sources, has been published in Fritz Mierau, ed., *Die Reiterarmee mit Dokumenten und Aufsätzen im Anhang* [*Red Cavalry*, with Documents and Criticism]. Sources for Babel's life are the several versions of his autobiography, his letters, and the memoirs of Nathalie Babel, Ilia Ehrenburg, Konstantin Paustovski, and others. See the bibliography for details.

[2] Babel's autobiography was first published in *Pisateli. Avtobiografii i portrety sovremennykh russkikh prozaikov* [Writers. Autobiographies and Portraits of Contemporary Russian Prose

Babel's several versions of his autobiography run altogether to no more than a few pages, scarcely sufficient evidence for reconstructing so complex and mysterious a man.

Many readers after reading Babel think that they know a great deal about his life. They fail to take into account his love of fiction. As more of the fragments of his life have come to light in recent years, we have been able to measure more precisely the distance between the facts of his experience and the re-creation of that experience in art.

The sources are all seriously flawed. Babel's letters, especially the largest available group, those to his mother and sister, show him laboring to present his chosen view of himself to others. In many cases the letters are distorted by the exigencies of communicating under the shadow of political surveillance. The memoirs of others reveal the biases of their authors. Thus the painter Yuri Annenkov shows Babel ready to take up émigré status in Paris in the thirties, while Ilia Ehrenburg shows a loyal, pro-Soviet Babel, the better to speed the process of "rehabilitation." The recollections of Paustovski, who knew Babel longest among the memoir writers, present special problems. Many of the anecdotes he tells are uncomfortably like recountings of Babel's stories. One wonders if Paustovski is using paraphrase as a means of acquainting readers with Babel's difficult-to-obtain works (a subterfuge common in Soviet

---

Writers], edited by V. Lidin. I refer to the text of this version as published in I. Babel, *Izbrannoe* [Collected Works], Moscow, 1966, pp. 23–24. A reworked version of the autobiography exists in manuscript form. (See *Izbrannoe*, p. 462, for details.)

criticism) or if perhaps Babel has practiced his mystification on Paustovski, trying out on him, in the guise of anecdotes from his past, versions of stories that he is working on.[3] These materials will be valuable when the time comes to write a true biography of Babel, but the scholar must have a solid foundation from which to judge the accuracy of the various views and accounts. At this point no such foundation exists. At best we can give an impressionistic account of Babel's life, fitting together in a mosaic a fragment from a letter here, a fragment from a memoir there to create a picture of the man. Such a picture will inevitably be incomplete.

If Babel were a petty litterateur, the kind of man whose work we read because he was of his times and whose life has meaning in the context of his times, what would we say of him? I am afraid we would say nothing at all. He is a man whose life had two great points of drama: his participation in the Civil War and his arrest in the Stalinist purges. But these events were common to the experience of the Soviet intelligentsia, and they are important to us only because we feel that the themes and attitudes of his work are bound up in ironic relationship with them.

Babel's private life was unhappy and chaotic, but again not so much so as to be truly exceptional. He was pressed for money, had difficulties with his wife, separated from

---

[3] Babel's sister has indicated that Paustovski's story of Babel's "elopement" with Eugenia Gronfein does not correspond to reality. As Judith Stora-Sandor remarks (p. 26), this is undoubtedly one of Babel's jokes.

her, became involved with other women, and tried to reunite his family; inevitably, his domestic affairs were en-
tangled in, and complicated by, political exigencies. He
had a sense of the roles he should play as son, husband,
and father, but found himself unable to play them satisfactorily because of his own inner conflicts and because of
the pressures of external affairs upon his private life.

He was a good companion to his friends, was convivial
and hospitable, a great wit. Although he knew Eisenstein,
Gorki, Maiakovski, and many other important artists and
writers of the twenties, he left no record that would illuminate the decade's literary scene. His brief reminiscences of
Gorki and Bagritski are not particularly helpful. They
show us more of Babel than of their subjects. Memoir was
not his forte. His impulse to give order to the materials, to
reduce and intensify, was too strong to allow him to be
an adequate medium for the real. His life has become the
stuff of the memoirists of his generation, but we have no
enriching view of his times from him.

Babel's life cannot have extraordinary meaning for us
except as it converges upon those important events that
exist in another order of reality, the artistic works. Ironically, the simple facts of his life always seem inadequate to
explain the remarkable complexity and depth of the works.
We lack a detailed record of Babel's consciousness apart
from his stories, but it was in the peculiar insular world of
his own mind that Babel's deepest and truest life was lived.
This fact constitutes the enigma that all who knew him
felt, the mystery of the other, hidden life. The works are

messages to us from that other life, the only record that we have.

Isaac Babel was born in 1894 in Odessa and was raised first in Nikolaev, a small town on the coast of the Black Sea, and later in Odessa. One gets a good sense of Babel's family background from the memoir of his daughter Nathalie. The father, Emmanuel, was a representative for a manufacturer of agricultural machinery and in time grew prosperous enough to set up his own dealership in Odessa. Emmanuel Babel was one of those colorful, energetic commercial men whose exuberance Babel evokes in the Odessa stories. Nathalie Babel writes of him, "Dandyish, elegant, good-looking, he was a man of imposing physique and impetuous nature. His rages were legendary." [4] Emmanuel Babel's considerable energy and worldly ambition were reflected in his expectations for his son.

Although there was also a daughter (Maria Emmanuelovna, called Mary, born in 1899), Isaac was the darling of the family. He seems to have enjoyed a comfortable and secure childhood, marred only by the excessive demands of his ambitious father, who imposed on him a formidable schedule of lessons. In 1905 young Babel was sent from Nikolaev to Odessa, where he lived for a year with his grandmother and two aunts while attending the Nicholas I Commercial School. (In the following year the entire Babel family returned to Odessa.) In addition to his regular studies, Babel was taught several foreign lan-

[4] Nathalie Babel, "Introduction," *The Lonely Years,* p. xvi.

guages and Hebrew and was enrolled in the famous "factory" of violinists, the school run by Peter Solomonovich Stoliarski where David Oistrakh was later to study. Babel writes in his autobiography, "I rested in school." The tradition of Babel's life insists upon his gift for languages (his perfect command of French would later impress French writers with whom he came in contact) and upon his lack of talent for the violin.

In his brief autobiography Babel makes two points about his upbringing, that it was Jewish and that his father made him study many subjects. The Babels, an upwardly mobile Jewish family, were moving away from strict adherence to Jewish custom. Judith Stora-Sandor, investigating the family's attitude toward Jewish culture, concludes that "the Babels, who at this period already belonged to the *moyenne bourgeoisie,* followed a path between two extremes with a marked tendency toward assimilation." [5] She notes the evolution in the family from the generation of the grandparents. Babel's paternal grandfather pursued rabbinical studies, and his paternal grandmother spoke Yiddish in the family and could speak Russian only with difficulty. Babel's parents spoke Yiddish to each other, but Russian to their children. Babel's sister Mary, who now lives in Brussels, speaks very little Yiddish. The same trend is noticeable in the observance of religious traditions: strict observance in the grandparents' generation, little observance in the grandchildren's. Babel's father, however, insisted that his son receive a Jewish education. He was sent to

⁵ Stora-Sandor, p. 19.

heder from the age of six and was tutored at home in Hebrew until the age of sixteen.

The emotional weight that Babel gave to each of the chief formative influences of his childhood is apparent from the way in which he later introduced them into his fiction. The family atmosphere meant security, but also confinement. The larger worlds of Odessa and literature meant danger, but also freedom. These worlds were concentrated in the experience of school as Babel describes it in his autobiography:

> The school was gay, rowdy, noisy and multilingual. There the sons of foreign merchants, the children of Jewish brokers, Poles from noble families, Old Believers and many billiard-players of advanced years were taught. Between classes we used to go off to the jetty at the port, to Greek coffee houses to play billiards, or to the Moldavanka to drink cheap Bessarabian wine in the taverns.

Babel gave the place of honor among the influences on his development to French literature and culture. He praised Monsieur Vadon, the French teacher at the Nicholas I Commercial School: "He was a Breton and, like all Frenchmen, possessed a literary gift. He taught me his language. From him I learned the French classics by heart and came to know the French colony in Odessa well. At the age of fifteen I began to write stories in French." Babel did not persist in writing in French, but declared his allegiance most strongly in his choice of a language and a subject matter for his writing. As Renato Poggioli has perceptively written: "Babel refused both Yiddish and Hebrew, and chose instead Russian, the idiom of the goyim. He did so not merely to escape from the ghetto, but to turn, through Russia, to Europe and the West." [6]

The evidence suggests that Babel, like many sensitive people when young, went through a period of undefined idealistic and religious enthusiasm. At ages fifteen and sixteen he belonged to a Jewish welfare organization that worked among the poor in Odessa. During his student years he was drawn to Tolstoyanism. Later he said to his French translator, Maurice Parijanine, "For a whole year I didn't read a line that hadn't been written by Tolstoy, and it was then that I came to understand all the sublime virtue of the Russian people." [7] Babel's Jewish studies led him also to an interest in the Hasidic movement with its emphasis on mystical communion between God and man.

Babel emerged from the sheltered life of the family in 1911 when he was sent by his father to the Institute of Financial and Business Studies in Kiev (the *numerus clausus* prevented his entering the University of Odessa).[8] In Kiev he was introduced into the family of Boris Gronfein, a well-to-do importer and manufacturer of agricultural machines who was a business friend of Babel's father. Here at the age of sixteen he met the household's youngest daughter, Eugenia, whom he was to marry in 1919. Nathalie Babel describes the elegant, cultivated life

[6] Renato Poggioli, *The Phoenix and the Spider*, p. 230.
[7] Stora-Sandor, p. 21.   [8] Nathalie Babel, p. xvi.

of the Gronfeins and their interest in Western culture. The family was very much a part of that larger, more liberated world toward which Babel strove. Young Eugenia was planning a career as an artist and lived wholly absorbed in the world of books and art. It is not surprising that young Babel was drawn to this girl, whose spiritual exaltation and youthful enthusiasm for the great works of Western culture matched his own. Babel came into contact with the Jewish intelligentsia of Kiev and published his first story in a Russian-language bimonthly. With the outbreak of World War I the Institute was moved to Saratov. By this time Babel had begun to examine the influence of the family milieu on his development, as is reflected in a sketch, "Childhood. At Grandmother's," dated November 12, 1915.

Two conflicting impulses shaped Babel's life as a whole. One impulse compelled him to break free from confinement, to move into a larger sphere, to seek increased freedom, to enjoy stronger sensations, to achieve greater success. The second impulse, reflecting a deep anxiety, compelled him to seek security, to draw into himself, to retreat to safety, and to limit his ambitions. Naturally the first of these impulses expresses itself most strongly in the exuberance of youth. Babel went directly to the country's literary capital, Petersburg, as soon as he was graduated from the Institute in December 1915. He seems to have been confident that he would succeed as a writer.

Babel later liked to describe his stay in Petersburg as a time of physical hardship and persecution. It may well be that to so young a man, who had led so secure a life, to be on his own in the great Russian capital seemed both adventurous and precarious, but his father still sent him money, and there is no evidence that he suffered hardship from living "illegally" in the city as a Jew. Babel gives us a hint of the true state of affairs: "About twenty years ago, I roamed the streets of St. Petersburg with faked documents in my pocket and wearing no overcoat in a ferocious winter. I did own an overcoat, I have to confess, but I didn't wear it on grounds of principle." [9]

Renato Poggioli's account of Babel's life demonstrates how well the wily Babel has been able to invest himself with the aura of heroism. Not only does Poggioli state that Babel was a "pauper" and "a denizen of the worst urban slums" but he asserts that "Babel lived in the capital illegally, without means of his own, and with great hardships, in order to start a literary career." [10] These were far from the actual circumstances of the comfort-loving Babel, who had found a room in the respectable, bourgeois family of a Petersburg engineer.

As far as his advancement as a writer goes, Babel not only did not suffer, but received unusual and early recognition with the publication of two of his stories by Maxim Gorki in his journal *The Chronicle*. This gave Babel entrée into the brilliant young circle gathered around *The Chronicle*, which included the young Futurists Brik, Shklovski, and Maiakovski. Viktor Shklovski has described the im-

---

[9] "Nachalo" [The Beginning], *Izbrannoe*, p. 315.
[10] Poggioli, p. 230.

pression made by Babel on these young sophisticates: "Everyone noticed Babel's story and remembered it. They now took note of Babel, too. Middle height, high forehead, big head, an unwriterly face, dressed in dark clothes, talks entertainingly." [11] In this same period Babel worked for the Petersburg newspaper *Journal of Journals*. In his brief reminiscence of his acquaintance with Gorki, Babel tells the story (which became a key part of the self-created legend) how Gorki sent him "to the people" to learn about life.[12] Whether this was the case, or whether he was led on by his own curiosity and desire to experience everything from which he had been excluded by the circumstances of his upbringing, Babel enlisted in the army in October 1917 and served briefly on the Rumanian front. According to Nathalie Babel, he was sent back to Odessa in 1918 after contracting malaria.[13] In any case he was once again in Petersburg by March 1918, working for Gorki's newspaper *New Life*. In his autobiography, Babel, indulging in that compression of detail with which he molded the story of his life to his own purposes, offers a long list of his activities during the revolution, including work in the Cheka and in the Commissariat of Education, and participation in the expeditions to the countryside in 1918 to collect food for the city. Babel also claimed to have

[11] "Kriticheskii romans" [A Critical Romance], *LEF*, no. 2, 1924, p. 152. Apparently Babel made Maiakovski's acquaintance at this time and became sufficiently friendly with him that Maiakovski later visited Babel in Odessa. See Babel's letter to his family on Apr. 27, 1930, *The Lonely Years*, p. 137.

[12] "Nachalo," p. 316. [13] Nathalie Babel, p. xviii.

fought against the Whites at the time of Judenich's attack on Petersburg. Whether or not he was actually involved in these activities has never been established.

In 1919, Babel married Eugenia Gronfein in Odessa and took a job as editor with the Ukrainian State Publishing House. But his return to Odessa, family, and domesticity was short-lived. In the early summer of 1920, he was sent by Sergei Ingulov, Secretary of the Party Committee in Odessa, as correspondent for IUGROSTA, the southern division of the national news service that was the predecessor of TASS. Traveling under the name Kiril Vassilevich Liutov to conceal his Jewish identity, Babel was assigned to Budenny's First Cavalry, where he worked for the Division newspaper, *The Red Cavalryman*.

Babel's tour of duty with the First Cavalry was the experience that he had been seeking. He wrote hack journalism for the propaganda sheet (the one example of the work of this period to survive shows Babel putting his talents as feature writer to use by turning out short sketches of the daily life in the division with an inspirational, upbeat tone),[14] but his primary interest was the diary in which he hoarded the anecdotes, scenes, sights, and impressions for the work he was going to produce later. Babel went into the Civil War consciously as a writer seeking materials. Apparently he plied his craft under fire. In the diary he mentions the manuscripts of stories that he carried about with him in the midst of battle and that, not surprisingly,

[14] "Ee den" [Her Day], *Literaturnoe nasledstvo*, vol. 74, p. 488.

he lost before the campaign was over. "I'm very sad about the manuscripts," he writes in the diary.

An unsent letter found between the pages of his diary gives a more personal glimpse of Babel's life in the First Cavalry than does the diary itself:

> As a heading today I have to write thus: edge of the woods, which is the old northwest Maidans. The staff headquarters of the division and the staff headquarters of the squadron have been here in the woods since morning. For whole days we travel from one brigade to another, observe the fighting, write summaries of operations, spend the nights in the woods, run away from airplanes which bomb us. The charming sky is above us, the sun is not hot, the pines sigh around us, hundreds of steppe horses whinny, oh to live here, but our thoughts are trained upon murder. My words sound stupid, but this war really is, though sometimes beautiful, in every way injurious.[15]

In the autumn of the same year Babel returned to Odessa in very poor health after the ordeals of the campaign. Here, in 1921, he became acquainted with the writer Konstantin Paustovski (later his protégé and lifelong friend). According to Paustovski, Babel was already a celebrated figure in Odessa at this time because of his works published in

[15] Quoted by L. Livshits in "Materialy k tvorcheskoi biografii I. Babelia" [Materials for a Critical Biography of I. Babel], *Voprosy literatury* [Problems of Literature], no. 4, 1964, p. 123.

Petersburg, because of his friendship with Maxim Gorki, and because of his tour of duty with the legendary Budenny. The "literary kids" (*literaturnye mal'chiki*) of Odessa followed him around, hanging on his every word. Older literary lights treated him with deference. To Odessites in these years Babel seemed to be the "first real Soviet writer," though he was still largely unknown on the national scene.[16]

Entering one of the most productive periods in his life, Babel found the key to developing his talent as a writer. From the start, he had been convinced of his vocation. Since 1915 he had been molding his life to prepare himself for the work he was certain he could produce. Yet when he returned to Odessa from Budenny's campaign, there was little to show for his talent and preparation. There was enough to convince undemanding admirers, to be sure, but Babel, never accepting standards lower than his own, placed little value on the work of his Petersburg days.

The next several years he spent in the south of Russia, where he laid the groundwork for two cycles of stories that would gain him national prominence, the Odessa stories and *Red Cavalry*. First Babel and his young wife lived together with Babel's family in a lively ménage that from time to time included Babel's mother-in-law. Later Babel went for his health (and possibly to find the peace to write) to the Caucasus, where he first traveled and later

[16] Konstantin Paustovski, *Povest' o zhizni* [Story of a Life], vol. 2, p. 326.

became a correspondent for the Tiflis newspaper *Dawn of the East*. Paustovski gives us a vivid if impressionistic account of these years in Babel's life: the somewhat frenzied *Gemütlichkeit* of a large Jewish household; the camaraderie among the young writers of Odessa, all nourishing hopes that in a surprising number of cases would be fulfilled; Babel's torments as a writer trying to meet nearly impossible standards of excellence.

Paustovski met Babel later while traveling in the Caucasus. He gives us several glimpses of the rather idyllic life Babel led in the exotic resort town of Batum, where he and his wife occupied a cabin perched on the side of a mountain. Before going to the Caucasus, Babel had already published one of the stories from what was to be the Odessa cycle, and now he was working on the first sketches of *Red Cavalry*, which were to appear in an Odessa newspaper at the beginning of 1923. Paustovski sensed beneath the calm exterior of their existence the developing estrangement between Babel and Eugenia.[17]

Early in 1923, Babel returned to Odessa, apparently at the request of his parents. Though his health was poor, he was still working on *Red Cavalry*, and had had several offers to publish it. He was thinking of moving to Moscow and awaited Gorki's return to Russia, hoping to consult him about the work.[18] The Odessa era of Babel's life came

[17] *Ibid.*, p. 506.
[18] See letter to I. L. Livshits (Apr. 17, 1923) and note, *Znamia* [The Banner], no. 8, 1964, p. 147.

to an end in 1923 with the death of his father in March and Babel's removal of the family to the village of Sergiev-Posad (now Zagorsk), outside Moscow.

Babel had been writing to friends from Odessa about his impatience to get to Moscow, which had become the center of the new postrevolutionary literary life. He was full of energy and ambition, buoyed up by the great creative surge he was experiencing. In his autobiography Babel writes: "Only in 1923 did I learn how to express my thoughts clearly and concisely. Therefore I consider that my literary career started at the beginning of 1924 when my stories 'Salt,' 'A Letter,' 'The Death of Dolgushov,' 'The King' and others appeared in volume four of Maia-kovski's magazine *LEF*." The appearance of the stories in *LEF* marked Babel's rise to prominence on the national literary scene. Konstantin Fedin wrote to Gorki in July 1924, "Babel is creating an uproar in Moscow. This fellow was in the cavalry for a long time and when he came back, he rained down a whole trunkful of manuscripts on the Moscow editorial offices and nearly drowned them. Everyone is ecstatic about him." [19] At the same time the *Pravda* reviewer wrote that Babel was "a rising star in our literature." [20] Subsequent stories from the *Red Cavalry* cycle were published in the journal *Red Virgin Soil*, edited by

[19] Konstantin Fedin, *Gorki sredi nas* [Gorki among Us], Moscow, 1967, p. 216. Fedin continues, "It seems that Zoshchenko ought to be insulted, since Babel has diluted him and introduced Odessisms into Sinebruikov's *skaz*."

[20] *Pravda*, no. 243, Oct. 24, 1924.

Voronski, and critical articles discussing Babel's work began to appear.

The literary scene in Moscow in the mid-1920's was volatile. A number of competing groups strove to gain control over the resources of literary life, which were now commanded by the government. Babel's stories became the focus of controversy among the groups. The controversy was initiated by none other than Semen Budenny, commander of the First Cavalry, who found Babel's depiction of his men insulting. A meeting was arranged at which the leading figures in Soviet literature discussed Babel's work, using it chiefly as a point of departure for discussing their own views on the nature of literature and its relationship to the "social command." [21] Neither Babel nor Budenny attended the meeting.

Babel's new notoriety did not prevent the State Publishing House from contracting to publish *Red Cavalry*, but it did create new obstacles for him, since he was asked to make extensive revisions in the stories. His editor was Dmitri Furmanov, already well known for his book about his tour of duty as political commissar with the legendary leader of the partisans, Chapaev. Babel's acquaintanceship with Furmanov opened on a note that was sounded frequently in his relationships with his editors. "Do not complain to me about the delay with *Red Cavalry*," he writes to Furmanov on December 12, 1924. "This delay will be of benefit to all three interested parties—the

---

[21] For a description of the meeting see L. K. Kuvanova, "Furmanov i Babel," *Literaturnoe nasledstvo*, vol 74, p. 500.

State Publishing House, the manuscripts and me." In conversation with Furmanov, Babel defended his approach to *Red Cavalry:* "I gave what I saw with Budenny. I see that I didn't touch on the political work, that there's a great deal in general about the Red Army that I didn't touch on. I'll get to that, if I'm able, later. But for me that part doesn't come out to be as solid as the part I've done. Obviously, everyone has his own thing." [22]

The eagerly anticipated Moscow period was a disaster for him. He had actually brought much less of *Red Cavalry* to Moscow in completed form than he dared to admit, and he was under the intense pressure of deadlines that were impossible to meet because of his painstaking method of work. At the same time other momentous changes were taking place in his life. The severe winter in Moscow seemed to aggravate his poor health. Early in 1925 he went to the Caucasus for a cure. Upon his return, Furmanov, who had heard that Babel was near death from asthma, found him healthy and blooming. Yet the writer S. J. Grigorev reported to Gorki in a letter in March 1926: "[Babel] has asthma. He says it's from a concussion. He plans his life on the assumption that he has five years to live." [23]

There is some evidence that the northern climate was harmful for Babel, as for Pushkin, in more ways than one. He seems to have been wearied by the polemical struggles

[22] *Ibid.*, p. 506–7. Kuvanova treats Babel's friendship for Furmanov in detail.
[23] *Literaturnoe nasledstvo*, vol. 70, p. 134.

going on in Soviet literature. He wrote to his sister, who had gone abroad to be married, "Like everyone in my profession, I am oppressed by the prevailing conditions of our work in Moscow; that is, we are seething in a sickening professional environment devoid of art or creative freedom." [24]

Money was always a major problem for Babel. He needed money to buy a respite for creative work, but the jobs he took to get money drained his energies. Babel was now working (as he was to work throughout his life) as a writer of scenarios for the films. He began by writing a scenario, "Benia Krik," based on his short story "The King." He worked on scenarios based on several stories by Sholom Aleichem. He also edited and translated French and Hebrew.

To add to his misery Babel now underwent the second of the major crises in confidence about his work that mark his career. He turned away from *Red Cavalry*, and began writing stories drawing upon the experiences of his childhood. Once again the crisis led Babel to reach a depth in his work he had not previously attained. "The Story of My Dovecot" was published in *Red Virgin Soil* in 1925. Babel wrote to his mentor Gorki, who had expressed thanks for the dedication of the story,

> At the beginning of the current year, after a year and a half of work, I began to have doubts about my writings. I found them mannered and florid. It seemed

[24] Letter of May 12, 1925. *The Lonely Years*, p. 61.

to me that I was entering a bad period. In Petersburg in 1917 I understood how great my incapacity was and "went to the people." I lived for six years among the people, and in 1923 again I took up literary work. I was tortured by the thought that I had failed to fulfill your expectations. But now you know that I did not grow lazy, did not give up writing, did not forget the words you said to me that first time in the office of *The Chronicle*.[25]

Babel often saw in his life a series of repeated patterns. He tended to ignore the facts that contradicted the pattern, as in this case he ignored the substantial amount of writing he did in the period 1917–1923. But he was accurate in the main point when he called attention to recurrent crises of confidence in his work.

In the same letter Babel asked Gorki to help him obtain a visa for Eugenia, who wanted to study painting in Italy. Babel had hoped to go abroad with his wife and his mother for his health, but now it was decided that he must stay in Moscow to attend to various projects and that he would join his wife later. In fact the marriage was breaking up, though Babel continued to cherish the idea for many years that he would reunite the family. At least part of the reason for the separation was a liaison that Babel had contracted with a woman in Moscow. Yet there is no evidence that either Babel or Eugenia regarded the separation as perma-

[25] Letter to Gorki of June 25, 1935. *Literaturnoe nasledstvo,* vol. 70, p. 38.

nent. She managed to get a visa for France and went to Paris in November 1925.

Babel was thus left alone with his mother, responsibility for whom weighed heavily upon him. He considered sending her abroad to his sister, but his mother disliked the idea of leaving Russia. Babel then pleaded with his sister to return to Russia and set up a home with their mother. He felt that he must free himself from the financial burdens that took time away from his writing. When he received no satisfactory reply, his letters became more desperate.

> Until you and Mama settle down somewhere definitely, I can't move from here. And I must get out of here. With every day, living in Moscow becomes more painful and unfruitful for me, and to stay on here indefinitely would be to invite both material and spiritual poverty.

> In spite of my many letters, you can't imagine the state of my affairs, which have become catastrophic and intolerable. I can't go anywhere and just abandon Mama to her fate. I can't rush off to Paris for a month or two and then dash back to Moscow for money that I can get only for work, and right now I'm so distracted and worn out I can't work.[26]

Finally it was decided that the mother would join her daughter in Belgium. This did free Babel to travel and

[26] Letters of Feb. 8 and March 22, 1926. *The Lonely Years,* pp. 69–70.

pursue his work, but it tended to make permanent the separation in the household that would subsequently cause Babel much suffering, worry, and financial embarrassment. If up to 1926 Babel's life was characterized by his adventurousness, his desire to move outward into the larger world, his search for new experience and adventure, then after 1926 a countertendency prevailed, a drawing in, an attempt to establish for himself an island of security in which he could live and work. During the severe emotional crises Babel underwent in 1925 and 1926, he seems to have willfully broken up his family in an attempt to assert his freedom.[27] This turned out to be a misreading of his own needs and desires that cost him dearly and that he never stopped paying for. Henceforth his search as an artist for the freedom to work unhindered by the demands made upon him by the outside world—Soviet officials, his family, those who commissioned work from him—becomes a key theme of his letters. Babel had the habit of hiding himself away to write, and he became ever more ingenious at finding places where he would work in isolation. After his mother's departure for Belgium in 1926 he found a quiet refuge and indulged his passion for horses by going to the Khrenovaia Stud Farm in Voronezh province. In the fall of 1926 he wrote his play *Sunset* in a rest home for writers near Moscow. The period of seclusion, rest, and productive work appears to have restored Babel's equilib-

[27] Nathalie Babel reports that Babel urged his wife to go abroad, though her "desire to travel was at first extremely nebulous" (*ibid.*, p. xxiv). The letters of 1926 to his sister show him almost desperate to dispose of the burden of responsibility for his mother.

rium. He wrote to his mother, "I am leaving for Kiev, where I will stay for quite a while because I would like to work in a quiet, secure atmosphere. Then I'll go abroad for quite a long time. I am liquidating the horrible 'Moscow period' of my life that has been so painful to me." [28]

The work on *Red Cavalry*, which was supposed to be completed by January 1925 according to Furmanov, was not done until well into 1926. In February 1926, Babel wrote to Furmanov that he was sending the corrected manuscript, but in March he was begging for the galley proofs so that he could make some "insignificant changes." Furmanov died that month without seeing *Red Cavalry* through the press. It was published before the end of the year. By this time a number of smaller editions had appeared that included stories from the Odessa and *Red Cavalry* cycles in various combinations.

Babel was delayed in his plans to travel abroad by the death of his father-in-law in March 1927, and by the necessity for dealing with the estate and taking care of his mother-in-law. Finally in August 1927, he was able to end the horrible Moscow period of his life with its nightmarish saga of troubles with relatives, financial difficulties, and artistic crises and to go abroad to France to join his wife, taking his mother-in-law with him. In a letter to a friend in Moscow he described his life as he found himself in France:

> I lead the most simple life. I write. I can't sit for
> more than three francs' worth in a cafe. I don't have

[28] Letter of Nov. 29, 1926. *Ibid.*, p. 84.

much money. There's nothing to have a good time on. I walk around the streets of Paris and look closely at everything. I avoid old acquaintances and don't look for new ones. I go to bed at eleven and that turns out to be late. In our street after ten o'clock you don't find a single lighted window.[29]

At the end of the year Babel visited Marseille, which he saw as "an Odessa that has flourished." [30]

Babel's trip to France did not save him from his troubles. His letters to his mother and sister in Belgium express the usual concerns about money, illness, and visas. Babel's health continued poor. He was writing again, but under the tension imposed by an agreement he had made with the magazine *Novyi mir*, which apparently paid him a regular allowance on the condition that he contribute regularly.[31] Babel, who was never able to work under pressure of a deadline, fills his letters with complaints about *Novyi mir*'s demands and the demands of others to whom he had made commitments. The failure of *Sunset* in a poorly staged production by the Moscow Art Theater No. 2 filled him with anger. Friends advised him that sinister rumors that he planned to stay abroad permanently were circulating in Moscow. Gorki was urging Babel to visit him in Sorrento, but the Italians would not give Babel a visa. He grew increasingly homesick for Russia, but he did not want to return "empty-handed," without the manuscripts to meet his commitments and free his future.

[29] Letter to A. G. Slonim, Oct. 4, 1927. *Znamia*, p. 156.
[30] Letter to I. L. Livshits, Oct. 28, 1927. *Ibid.*, p. 149.
[31] Letter to A. G. Slonim of July 31, 1928. *Ibid.*, p. 156.

In spite of his difficulties Babel found time early in 1928 to work on a project for which he had great hopes. He wrote to I. L. Livshits in January, "Again, as in the days of my youth, I am planning a *coup d'état* in my literature. We'll see if it turns out well." [32] In February he wrote to Gorki, "I am finishing a damned book that I can't get out of and then I'm going to throw myself into the world again to take the fresh air." [33] In the same week he wrote to a friend in Moscow, "Up to February I worked properly. Then I undertook to write one completely amazing thing. Yesterday evening at 11:30 I discovered that it is completely trash and bombastic to boot. A month and a half of life wasted for nothing." [34] After this fiasco he determined that he would not rush his work and sent an angry letter to *Novyi mir* reproaching the magazine for pressing him. In this letter he spoke of a new plan: he would find a job independent of his literary work that would allow him to write at his leisure.[35]

In September 1928, Babel returned to Russia, at least partly in order to resolve complications over the legacy received by his wife on the death of her father. Eugenia stayed in Paris to look after her mother, for whom no other provision could be made at that time. Babel hoped to go abroad again in 1929 to be with Eugenia, who was pregnant, but he was unable to obtain permission from the Soviet authorities. This was partly due to a scandal caused

[32] Letter of Jan. 10, 1928. *Ibid.*, p. 150.
[33] Letter of Feb. 29, 1928. *Literaturnoe nasledstvo,* vol. 70, p. 40.
[34] Letter to L. V. Nikulin, Feb. 24, 1928. *Znamia*, p. 153.
[35] Letter to V. P. Polonski, July 31, 1928. *Ibid.*, p. 156.

by the appearance, in the Polish weekly *Literary News*, of an interview made with Babel by the Polish poet Alexander Dan during Babel's stay on the Riviera. Dan attributes to Babel views highly critical of the Revolution and of Soviet power. Babel's language as Dan records it sounds spurious, and Babel subsequently denied having made critical statements and cleared himself to the satisfaction of the authorities in 1930. Nevertheless, he was unable to get permission to return to France until September 1932.

In the meantime he traveled widely in the Ukraine and the south of Russia, gathering impressions for his writing and looking for a haven. His combat with Polonski, editor of *Novyi mir*, continued, and it was only in 1931 that he could send the magazine a few stories "written several years ago and redone (comparatively) in the last few months." He was still engaged in writing what he considered to be a major work, but the nature of that work is not apparent from his letters.

Gorki had come forward belatedly to defend Babel against the charges of Budenny, comparing *Red Cavalry* to Gogol's *Taras Bulba*. This reopened the polemic, causing Budenny to reply to Gorki in an open letter, where among other things he accused Babel of having never seen any real fighting and suggested that *Red Cavalry* should be called "In the Backwaters of the *Red Cavalry*." [36] The Budenny letter sounds like a story narrated by one of

[36] For an English translation of the letter and Gorki's response see *The Lonely Years*, pp. 384–389.

Babel's Cossacks; no doubt it was his perception of this that caused Babel to write to his family, "I . . . was terribly tickled by it, even swelled up with glee." [37] Gorki replied to Budenny in a letter, which ended, "You are not right, Comrade Budenny. You are mistaken." According to Ervin Sinkó, Gorki requested that Stalin put an end to the controversy, and Stalin responded by dropping the right words at the right time: *"Red Cavalry* is not so bad as all that. It is a very good book." [38]

It seems that not all of the soldiers of the First Cavalry shared Budenny's distaste for Babel. In March 1929, Babel traveled to Kislovodsk in the Caucasus for a reunion with his "combat pals" from the First Cavalry. At the same time he visited Dmitri Schmidt, his friend from the First Cavalry who was now Director of the Krasnodar Cavalry School.[39]

With the birth of his daughter Nathalie in Paris, in July 1929, Babel's efforts to reunite his family in Russia intensified. Despite his wish to avoid Moscow and its baleful memories, he returned there to straighten out his affairs. In June 1930, he took a job as secretary of the village soviet at Molodenovo, about thirty miles from Moscow, and settled down in the house of the shoemaker, where he lived in

[37] *Ibid.,* p. 106.

[38] Ervin Sinkó, *Roman eines Romans* [A Novel about a Novel], translated by Edmund Trugly, Jr., p. 315.

[39] According to S. Tregub, Dmitri Schmidt was the prototype for Matthew Pavlichenko. Tregub describes Schmidt's enthusiasm for *Red Cavalry,* which he used as a text in classes that he taught for illiterate workers after the Civil War. (Untitled article, *Literaturnaia Rossiia* [Literary Russia], March 13, 1964.)

great austerity. Here at last he found the peace of mind to write. He continued to take a critical view of all of his past work and to look forward to the completion of the project on which he was embarked. His main concern was to fulfill his commitments to publishers so that he could get permission to go to France and see his daughter for the first time. In spite of the disorder in his affairs Babel's letters from Molodenovo have an air of serenity. In May 1931, Babel met Gorki again, for the first time in over a decade, when Gorki made one of his periodic trips to the USSR. "We felt all our former affection on meeting each other," Babel wrote to his family.[40] Gorki settled for a time near Molodenovo, and Babel was able to visit him freely. He wrote to his family, "Our relationship, formed in my youth, hasn't changed to this day." [41]

In late 1931 and early 1932 Babel published a number of stories in various periodicals, which apparently freed him to travel abroad, though again not before having to make strenuous efforts to overcome all kinds of difficulties. In March he arranged to get an apartment in Moscow, on the grounds that he planned to bring his family back from abroad. In September 1932 he left for France.

The reunion did not put an end to Babel's troubles. His financial situation was bleak. Yuri Annenkov, whom Babel often visited during his trips to Paris, remarked the change in Babel: the gay exterior he usually presented to outsiders had given way to gloom. In November, not long after his

[40] Letter of May 24, 1931. *The Lonely Years*, p. 174.
[41] Letter of July 7, 1931. *Ibid.*, p. 181.

arrival in France, Babel wrote to Annenkov, "Because of my stupidity I live badly. I am tormented by tedious receptions, by demands to give speeches and to compose foolish articles. Today I flew into a rage and decided to become a free citizen in the next two days." [42] According to Annenkov, Babel decided not to return to the Soviet Union.

But Babel was now to get a glimpse of the problems of supporting himself and his family in France. He contracted to write a scenario of *Red Cavalry* for a French film company, but refused to make the compromises required by the director and so was not paid for it. His debts continued to mount.

In April and May 1933, Babel took another step that may have been instrumental in his decision to return to the Soviet Union. He paid a visit to Gorki at Sorrento, where he read the draft of his play *Maria*, which he had been working on in Paris. Gorki was preparing at the time to return to Russia. Apparently Gorki made efforts on behalf of his protégé, which led to what Babel terms "very tempting offers from Moscow." The enticement seems to have been combined with at least a veiled threat. At the end of July, Babel wrote to bid Annenkov farewell: "I've received a strange summons from Moscow. I'm going in the most dramatic circumstances, without money, in debt." [43]

[42] Yuri Annenkov, *Dnevnik moikh vstrech* [A Diary of My Encounters], vol. 1, p. 305.
[43] *Ibid.*, p. 307.

Babel returned to Moscow to discover that "all sorts of absurd but sinister rumors have been circulating about me." [44] He managed to get away from the city, which was an evil talisman for him, by going to the Caucasus on assignment. The Caucasus as always turned out to be the best restorer of his spirits. He became friends with Betel Kalmykov, the energetic representative of Soviet power in the north Caucasus, whom he described as "a Kabardian by descent and by nature a great New Man. . . . He has been famous for a decade and a half already, but all the stories are easily outdone by reality." [45] Babel's letters describe a life of boar hunting and wandering in the steppes and mountains. He moved to a Cossack settlement, where he finished *Maria* and started a new play. As always his thoughts turned to his wife and daughter and to how he might, through his work, buy a reunion with them and achieve a permanent solution to their difficulties.

Babel was much concerned at this time about the general decline in the artistic quality of Soviet literature. He began to take advantage of the public appearances obligatory for a Soviet writer to teach his colleagues the standards of their craft. In 1934, before the First Congress of Soviet Writers, he gave a speech entitled "Our Enemy Is Triviality" in which he reminded his fellow writers of the necessity for respect for the reader. In a letter to his mother he wrote, "In a country as united as ours it is quite inevitable that a certain amount of thinking in clichés should appear and I want to overcome this standardized way of thinking

[44] Letter of Sept. 1, 1933. *Ibid.*, p. 239.
[45] Letter of Dec. 4, 1933. *Ibid.*, p. 244.

and introduce into our literature new ideas, new feelings
an rhythms." [46]

Maria was read at the Vakhtangov Theater and went into
rehearsal, but encountered strong criticism. Increasingly,
Babel was finding himself the center of intolerable controversy when he did not produce and intolerable controversy when he did. In spite of the response to *Maria* when
it was finally published (but not staged), Babel continued
to work on his new play.

In 1935 chance intervened to give Babel another op-
portunity to visit his family abroad. A Congress for the
Defense of Culture and Peace, which was to present a
united front of intellectuals against Fascism, was arranged
in Paris. The French writers demanded to know why Babel
and Pasternak had not been included in the Soviet delega-
tion. They were sent on several days after the Congress had
begun. Babel distinguished himself by delivering a speech
in French extemporaneously.[47] This brief visit of several
weeks' duration was the last time he was to spend with his
family. Before leaving for Paris he confided to a friend that
if his wife refused to return to Russia, he would begin
another family. His wife did not return with him.

After 1935, in the hostile and confining atmosphere of
Stalinist Russia, Babel drew more and more into himself.
He began living with a woman he had met in the early
1930's, Antonina Nikolaevna Pirozhkova, to whom a
daughter, Lidia, was born in January 1937. If Babel's marriage to Eugenia Gronfein was symptomatic of his attrac-

[46] Letter of June 13, 1935. *Ibid.*, p. 283.
[47] Nathalie Babel, p. xxv,

31

tion to the world of Western art and culture, his choice of a second wife was expressive of his loving acceptance of Russia. Antonina Nikolaevna was a fair, energetic woman, the daughter of an exiled intellectual, who had grown up in Siberia. Trained as an engineer, she worked on many of the great construction projects of the 1930's and, indeed, supported herself (and her daughter until she grew up) until her recent retirement by teaching at an engineering institute.

The death of Gorki in 1936 was a severe blow to Babel and increased his isolation. He lost not only a close friend and mentor, but a protector. Gorki's death made it all the more unlikely that he would be permitted to travel abroad again. In these years he was visited by many people, among them Gide and Malraux, but these visitations were just a distraction for him from his work. He hid himself away more frequently. Again he undertook work on film scenarios in order to buy the time to complete the book with which he had been struggling for many years.

Mundblit describes how in the line of work on the editorial board of *The Banner* he encountered Babel in the late thirties. Babel was up to his old tricks (by now he was the master of them) of extracting advances from publishers for one work in order to gain time for himself to work on another. Thus, Babel had at the expense of *The Banner* bought himself enough time to complete the story "Di Grasso." [48] The story was published in *Ogonek*, from which no doubt Babel had also received advances.

[48] G. Mundblit, "Isaak Emmanuilovich Babel'. (Iz vospominanii)," *Znamia*, no. 8, 1964, pp. 166–174.

Babel's letters are full of complaints that he could not become a "professional," by which he meant that he could not write regularly, to a prescribed length and to meet a deadline. His own standards of excellence became a painful burden for him, and yet he could not surrender them. The letters of the last years indicate that he came near to finishing the book on which he had labored for so long. The last letter to his mother and sister contain the lines, "Soon I will get to the finishing touches of my cherished Work. I expect to give it to the publishers by autumn." [49]

Even though Babel published relatively little and that sporadically, he continued to enjoy to a surprising degree the privileges available to leading Soviet writers. His work was sought for publication, he lived well by Soviet standards, and he was given a villa in the writer's colony at Peredelkino. It was here in 1939 that the Stalinist purges finally caught up with him. He was arrested in Peredelkino on May 15, 1939. His papers and manuscripts, including his nearly completed book, were taken and have not been found. According to Soviet official sources, he died in a labor camp on March 17, 1941. In the period following Stalin's death, Babel, along with many other victims of the purges, was "rehabilitated." The sentence was revoked, he was cleared of criminal charges, and the way was opened for republication of his works.

[49] Letter of May 10, 1939. "Vyderzhki iz pisem I. E. Babelia k materi i sestre," *Vozdushnye puti. Al'manakh,* vol. 3, p. 113.

2. Babel's Artfulness

"No iron can pierce the human heart so chillingly as a period, properly placed," Babel wrote in a line that was to become famous. Here Babel makes an assertion about the nature of the relationship between reader and writer that recurs in all his statements on writing and that illuminates the unusual nature of his stories: the writer is engaged in attacking the reader. Babel stated this more explicitly in answer to a question about his method of work: "I set myself a reader who is intelligent, well educated, with sensible and severe standards of taste. . . . Then I try to think how I can deceive and stun the reader." [1] This recalls Picasso's idea that a work of art should not be *trompe l'oeil* but *trompe l'esprit*.

The Babel story becomes a game between author and reader. Babel has anticipated the reader's responses to each of his moves. Herein lies his artfulness. The story takes its form from the strategy directed against the reader. Babel's stories are often "unpsychological" in their depiction of

[1] "O tvorcheskom puti pisatelia" [About the Writer's Creative Development] (stenogram of a conference at the Union of Soviet Writers on Sept. 28, 1937), *Nash Sovremennik* [Our Contemporary], no. 4, 1964, p. 100.

characters who tend to be, as one critic wrote, "verbal masks," but they are profoundly psychological in their manipulation of the reader.

Babel's reader has to undergo much. The stories are full of brutal events, murder, rape, all lethally aimed at him. Shock tactics are a way of catching him off guard or of breaking down his defenses. He feels uneasy and threatened, as well he might. Yet playfulness is as important to the game as attack. The reader is invited to join the author at his game. If we take the author's advice, we must be both serious and playful. We must assume that the story has a point and meaning which will make the game worthwhile for that gifted reader whom Babel proposes as his opponent; but if we are too earnest, we will miss the tricks. Babel calls for an unusual combination of attitudes and abilities. The reader must read the story as if it were a thriller and as if he were on the trail of the murderer, and he must at the same time not slight the paradoxical and complex views of justice and art that are Babel's themes.

The manipulation of the reader's responses as a formal device can be seen in a simple story from *Red Cavalry*, "The Remount Officer." [2] It opens with a move to engage

[2] Except where otherwise noted, all quotations from Babel's work are translated from *Izbrannoe* [Selected Works], published in 1966 by the Izdatel'stvo "Khudozhestvenaia literatura," Moscow. This most comprehensive collection of Babel's work yet published is generally available in libraries. The texts of *Red Cavalry* and of most of the stories in this edition follow the texts of the 1936 edition edited by Babel. Changes from earlier versions are noted where pertinent. Translations are mine.

the reader's sympathies: "A moan rises in the village." A two-sentence explanation follows: "The cavalry is trampling the grain and changing horses. In exchange for worn-out hacks the cavalry takes draft horses." The explanation pursues the emotional line suggested by the opening sentence. The neutral act of changing horses is colored by its association with "trampling the grain," a negative and destructive act, and this negative association is reinforced by the next sentence, which suggests a patent injustice in the whole business. The paragraph ends abruptly with a reversal and a definite judgment. "No one is to blame. You can't have an army without horses." The first paragraph thus circumscribes the complete movement of the story that is to come and anticipates the judgment that the story offers upon the events it describes.

An act is at the center of every Babel story, an act calling for judgment. The reader is prepared to judge. He has his own ideas about what is what. If he is to be made to attend to the act as something beyond his usual range of experience, requiring special standards of judgment, then Babel must trick him into giving his attention. Here Babel begins by appealing to the reader's natural sympathy for the downtrodden peasant whose livelihood is at stake. The surprising judgment at the end of the paragraph warns the reader that he must not take anything for granted, that his initial response may be inadequate.

Having alerted the reader to the complications of judgment in this story, Babel now returns to the initial problem, the injustice done to the peasants. It is true that whatever

36

the objective interpretation of the cavalry's act, "this knowledge doesn't make the peasants feel any better." Here
Babel advances a second claim on the peasants' behalf, one
more important than the claim of property, the claim of
outraged sensibilities. "The peasants, deprived of their
livelihood, feeling a welling up of bitter bravery and knowing that that bravery won't last for long, hasten to inveigh
without the slightest hope against the command, against
God and their pitiful lot." The outrage is reinforced by the
indifference of the Commander Zh., one of the many
"officers in full uniform" in Babel's stories who listen unmoved to the outcries of the victimized

But no sooner has Babel reasserted guilt than he hastens
to redress the balance by explaining Zh.'s indifference.
"Like every disciplined and exhausted worker, he knows
how in the spare minutes of existence to cut off the working
of his mind completely. In these few minutes of blessed
unconsciousness the chief of our staff winds up his worn-
out machine." Thus Babel in turn engages our sympathy for
this overworked officer who is after all only doing his duty.
The story has reached a stalemate. Any judgment seems
impossible. The balance between claims seems perfect.

After the first paragraph, which is serious and straightforward in tone, a sly irony has crept in. The result is to
turn the reader's attention away from the seriousness of the
peasant's plight. Lionel Trilling has pointed out in his introduction to Babel's stories that it would be a mistake to
dismiss what Babel is saying by referring to his irony. Irony
is often employed in Babel to redirect the reader's response

from an easy and sentimental sympathy to a more complicated emotion. The turn to irony in this story prepares the way for the concentration of attention on the central figure, Diakov.

The balance is disturbed by the arrival of Diakov, the new element who will be decisive in the judgment of the case. With his arrival the case is moved to a higher court: "There galloped up to the porch on his fiery Anglo-Arab Diakov, former circus gymnast and now remount officer, red faced, gray-mustached, wearing a black cloak and wide red trousers with silver stripes down the sides." The irreconcilable contest between two equally victimized opponents becomes a demonstration of virtuosity, a tour de force in which superior artistry claims its own. As Diakov gallops up to the porch, one of the horses received by the peasants in the exchange falls to the ground. The peasants, who have gotten no satisfaction from the chief of staff, now try the same tactics on Diakov. There follows one of those verbal duels so frequent in Babel's work. The peasant attacks with his pathetic note: "There, Comrade Officer, there's what your friends give us. See what they give us? Just try to farm with her." But Diakov conquers the peasant with his superior rhetoric, as he will soon conquer the horse with his superior skill:

> "For that horse, my good friend, you have full right to receive from the remount division 15,000 rubles, and if that horse were just a bit sprightlier, then in that case, my good friend, you could receive 20,000

rubles from the remount division. As for the horse falling, that's not a fact. If the horse falls and gets up, then it's a horse. If, to put it the other way round, it doesn't get up, then it's not a horse. But, by the way, this excellent filly will get up for me."

The peasant makes his final, most heartrending plea: "O, Lord, oh, merciful mother. . . . How can she get up, the poor orphan? She'll die . . . the poor orphan." But once again Diakov makes a telling thrust: "You're insulting the horse, friend. . . . Why, you're taking the horse's name in vain, friend." Diakov's rhetoric cleverly reverses things so that it is the peasant who is guilty toward the horse.

The reader's attention has now been completely redirected and the emotions drawn upon by the story changed. It is clear that any judgment based on sympathy cannot go against the peasants, for they have suffered very real injustices, being deprived of their livelihood and being ignored in their just complaints, which any reader can readily recognize and sympathize with. But the reader is no longer interested in the peasants' plight. His full attention is directed toward Diakov. In the longest paragraph of this two-page story Babel fulfills the expectation that Diakov will do something to justify that attention. Babel begins by creating an image of Diakov's physical splendor and prowess. "He nimbly swung his well-built athlete's body from the saddle. Straightening his splendid legs, caught at the knee by a strap, elegantly and nimbly as if on the stage, he went over to the dying animal." The general injustice to the peasants has now been narrowed to the specific and concrete suffering of the horse:

> It sorrowfully fixed its solid deep eye upon Diakov, and licked from his crimson palm some kind of invisible command. And immediately the exhausted horse felt the strength to act flowing from that gray, flourishing and swaggering Romeo. Raising its muzzle and slipping on its unsteady legs, feeling the impatient and commanding tickle of the whip under its belly, the nag slowly, attentively stood on its legs.

And the strength flowing from virtuosity that so affects the old nag in her dying moments affects the spectators who have unconsciously formed a ring in which the act can take place:

> And then we all saw how a fragile wrist in a fluttering sleeve caressed the dirty mane and how the whip with a moan pressed against her flanks that flowed with blood. Trembling all over, the nag stood on her own four feet and did not move her doggish, fearful loving eyes from Diakov.

The cruelty that is an inseparable part of Diakov's mastery is borne by the mare out of love inspired by his mastery. Thus is the balance tipped against the peasants as well, for Diakov's rare demonstration has become the payment for any injustice they may have suffered. Diakov makes the point. " 'That means it's a horse,' said Diakov to the peasant and added gently: 'And you complained, dear friend.' " Diakov's "dear friend" includes the peasant for a moment in intimacy with his splendid person. Just as Diakov's demonstration of artistry and power counters the injustice to the peasant of the appropriation of his horse, so this moment of intimacy erases the injustice of the chief of staff's indifference. The peasant's complaint has been taken note of in full measure. Diakov has exercised his full resources to respond to it. The chief injustice, the injustice to sensibilities, has been erased. "Throwing the reins to the orderly, the remount officer took the four steps at one jump and, flicking his opera cloak, disappeared into the staff building."

If we take Diakov's act out of context, it is easy enough to say that Babel treats this virtuosity with irony. But if we look at the careful articulation of the story, at the way its whole form focuses upon the moment of Diakov's triumph, at the powerful passage in which Diakov's "fragile wrist in a fluttering sleeve" caresses the "flanks that flowed with blood," then we must admit that the story is a psychological weapon directed at the reader to force him to attend to the claims of Diakov's virtuosity. "The Remount Officer" is a simple story. The opposition set up is a simple one. Babel relies for his effect on the act, which is so stunning as to require no further support. Only Diakov's past as a circus performer gives the shabby surroundings of the village a momentary glamor. Other stories are more expansive in their suggestiveness, but the fundamental structure remains the same.

The emphasis on the artist as strategist affects Babel's

work at every level.[3] In the parts of Babel's diary from the Polish campaign and the rough plans for *Red Cavalry* that have survived, we see Babel working out the strategies for his stories.[4] It is clear from these materials that Babel found a style for the work before he found a form for the materials. It is a style suggested by the diary form—laconic and without transitions. In his rough plans we find notes interspersed to himself: "No conclusions. Painstaking choice of words." "Short. Dramatic." "Very simple, setting forth the facts [*fakticheskoe izlozhenie*] without superfluous descriptions." Again he notes, "Short chapters, saturated with content." He jots down phrases to be used in the story. "Shivering in corridors, I have seen many nights, but such a damp, boring, dirty night I have not seen." We see developing in these plans a style, a rhythm which corresponds to those of the completed stories of *Red Cavalry*. The emphasis is already on the nature of the effect to be achieved.

The rough plans that have survived represent a stage in the work on *Red Cavalry* when Babel had not yet decided on the form the individual stories or the cycle was to take.

[3] For a discussion of how it affects Babel's style see J. van der Eng, "La description poétique chez Babel." Van der Eng is alone among the commentators on Babel in showing the function of style in giving structure to the stories.

[4] Parts of the diary have been published in German translation in Fritz Mierau, ed., *Die Reiterarmee mit Dokumenten und Aufsätzen im Anhang*, pp. 183–204. The rough plans for *Red Cavalry* ("Iz planov i nabroskov k Konarmii") were published in *Literaturnoe nasledstvo*, vol. 74, pp. 490–499.

None of these plans directly corresponds to any single story in *Red Cavalry*, though much of the detail is used. The plans show him thinking of a series of short chapters to be centered in an event. He numbers off subjects for chapters for an episode to be entitled "The Battle at Brody." He makes notes for another series to be called "The Battle at Lwow." Searching for a structure for the materials, he makes a note for himself, "By days." The plans are interspersed with underlined questions to himself concerning form: "Plots?" "Form?" "A story?" He thinks of writing a "poem in prose" about an episode involving books.

The most interesting thing about the plans is the richness of their detail. They give us some sense of how much material Babel came to sacrifice to his idea of form. The diary and rough plans teem with figures and observations that he never made use of. Yet at the same time he seems to have had an almost mystical regard for accuracy of detail and was reluctant to change even the names of characters. Many of the actual names (Prishchepa, Kolesnikov, Grishchuk) are preserved in the *Red Cavalry* stories. Others (Melnikov, Timoshenko) were changed after first publication (to Khlebnikov and Savitski).

Babel is noted for his painstaking revision of his work. Paustovski reports that Babel once showed him a great sheaf of papers that turned out to be the twenty revisions of the story "Liubka Cossack." Comparison of the various published editions show Babel still at work refining the style of the stories, eliminating unnecessary adjectives, cutting away too-explicit symbolism.[5] Often he seems to be following Hemingway's dictum that a writer can cut anything from a story as long as he knows what it is.[6] In the rough plans for *Red Cavalry* we see a more fundamental process of revision. The plans show him juggling details, names, phrases, bits of scenery around from story to story. Details become discrete units that can be fitted into the mosaic of the story. He tries a phrase in several variations: "Proigral ia tebia, Sasha" ("I lost you, Sasha") changes in the next plan to "Proigral ia tebia, Pava," and finally turns up in *Red Cavalry* in another context when Khlebnikov says to the commander in "Story of a Horse," "Proigral ty menia, voenkom." ("You lost me, Commander.")

This detachment of details from their original contexts

[5] Between first publication of "Pan Apolek" in *Krasnaia nov'* [Red Virgin Soil] (no. 7, 1923), and last publication, done under his supervision in the 1936 *Rasskazy*, Babel made nearly thirty changes in the seven-page story.

[6] Ehrenburg reports Hemingway's admiration for Babel's style: "He had just read Babel for the first time and said, 'I have never believed that arithmetic is important for the appreciation of literature. I have been criticized for writing too concisely, but I find that Babel's style is even more concise than mine, which is more wordy. It shows what can be done. Even when you've got all the water out of them, you can still clot the curds a bit more.'" From "A Speech at a Moscow Meeting in Honor of Babel, November 11, 1964," in *You Must Know Everything: Stories 1915–1937*, translated by Max Hayward and edited by Nathalie Babel, p. 235.

and the recombination of them in new contexts result in the abstraction of the details. They cease to be realistic and descriptive, "copied from life," and come to function as symbolic units in the stories. The development of Babel's style depends upon this abstraction, for once the detail had ceased to be attached to the realistic description of an actual event, it came to function as part of the affective design of the work, as a counter in the psychological game Babel wages with his readers.

Thus Babel comes to structure through style.[7] Paustovski reports Babel saying:

> "What holds my things together? What sort of cement? They really should fall apart at the slightest touch. Sometimes in the morning I start to write about a small thing of no importance, some trifling detail or other, and by evening it's turned into an elaborate tale." He answered his own question by saying that his stories were held together by their style only, but then he would laugh at himself: "Who's going to believe that a story can be made just by style—without content, or plot, or suspense? What sheer nonsense." [8]

[7] For a discussion of the structure of Babel's stories see Victor Terras, "Line and Color: The Structure of I. Babel's Short Stories in *Red Cavalry*," pp. 141–156. Many of Terras's general comments are useful, though he is less helpful when it comes to interpreting individual stories.

[8] Konstantin Paustovski, "A Few Words about Babel," in *You Must Know Everything*, p. 281.

Flaubert has written, "Style in itself is already a perfect method of seeing things." [9] When Babel finds a means of giving unity to the fragments of his experience, it is through point of view, through the way things are seen. From the earliest published work we find a consistent search for a "voice" appropriate to the subject matter. Later "voice" becomes the chief way of distinguishing styles, that is, of creating stories. The voice becomes the story. We attend to its tone more than to what it is saying. It is the cement that holds the fragments together, that gives a surface to the story. Babel's stories come to depend upon the situating of masklike or emblematic figures in a landscape or architectural space, the whole illuminated and held together by the binding power of point of view. The combination of mosaic-like fragments abstracted from context and the steady illumination of style gives the stories an enigmatic and static quality. [10]

The extraordinary economy of a Babel story demands that every phrase be put to use, that nothing be wasted. The characteristic structure is an anecdote preceded by other materials that serve to "place" the anecdote and to

[9] Letter to Luise Collet of Jan. 16, 1852, *Correspondance*, Deuxième série (1847–1852) (Paris, 1926), p. 346.

[10] See Robert Melville on the painter Henri Rousseau: "We can abstract from *The Sleeping Gypsy* a recipe for the enigma in painting: it is the situating of utterly still, imperturbably self-contained figures in a purely formal relationship which contrives nevertheless to simulate the appearance of an encounter." "Rousseau and Chirico," *Scottish Art and Letters*, no. 1, 1944. Quoted by Roger Shattuck in *The Banquet Years* (New York: Vintage Books, 1968).

give it resonance. Sometimes it is followed by what the Formalist critics liked to call a "kontsovka," a formula for ending a work, but often it simply ends as soon as the point is made, as the spending of the energy of narration brings things to equilibrium. The reader, unaccustomed to the density of the very short form, is tempted to leap ahead to the anecdote, to the "story," ignoring the opening lines that would prepare him for the story's reception, and is apt to be left aghast as the "story" ends almost immediately. Babel's work is best appreciated by the sensibility that has a wide experience of lyric poetry. He requires an attentiveness to detail and a capacity for responsiveness to lyric economies of expression that are well developed usually only in the reader of poetry. This quality, among others, connects him to the avant-garde period.

Joseph Frank has written of the novels of the avant-garde period that they are distinguished by a striving for "spatial form," by a desire to overcome the limitations of narrative that unfolds in time and to achieve the instantaneous impact of painting.[11] Babel's work is particularly visual in its impact.[12] His parable about his own art is transferred to a

[11] "Spatial Form in Modern Literature," in *The Widening Gyre* (New Brunswick, New Jersey: Rutgers University Press, 1963), pp. 3–60.

[12] Yuri Annenkov reports in his memoirs (*Dnevnik moikh vstrech*) that Babel was especially interested in painting and talked with him more often about it than about literature. See also Eisenstein's comment reported by V. Demin: "At that time Eisenstein dropped the significant comment that in Babel's stories he found 70 per cent of what he needed as a director, while in

47

painter, Pan Apolek. The stories are "spatial," too, in Frank's special sense. Each must be held in the head and "read" in an instant. They are whole units that can only be understood as whole units—as instantaneous and complete apprehensions of experience. The Babel story is a carefully limited space, a canvas into which he paints the significant word-objects before our eyes. As they emerge we recognize them and say, "Ah, a church!" "Ah, a man!" But having "recognized" the elements of the story, we have not yet understood the story. To understand we must take note of the significant relationships that exist among the objects in the space Babel has created to contain them. Babel has proposed a game in which the reader must take an active part. In spite of the affective power of the stories there is a coolness behind them. Our final impression of them is of order, control, and precision.[13] The reader is invited to examine his emotions. The last response to the story, if we are to follow it to its fullest range, must be an intellectual one. This imposition of the cool intellectual tone upon the shocking emotional one creates that special tone of voice which seems uniquely Babelian to us, an equilibrium achieved by the masterful balancing of opposed forces.

The extraordinary economy and condensation of Babel's

Babel's scenarios he found only 30 per cent." (*Film bez intrigi* [A Film without a Plot], Moscow, 1966, p. 103.)

[13] Babel said to Paustovski: "A comparison must be as exact as a slide rule and as natural as the smell of dill. All parentheses and punctuation must be handled properly with a view to the maximum effect of the text on the reader and not according to a dead catechism. Lines in prose must be drawn firmly and cleanly as on an engraving." (*Povest' o zhizni*, p. 328.)

stories create the danger that neatness and precision will destroy the power of the work. Babel escapes the confines of the very short form (Lionel Trilling has wisely given the stories the label "short fictions" to escape the problem of definition; Babel called the works "miniatures" and "novellas") by turning to the cycle, which is loose and expansive in structure. The cycle is never completed. It can always be added to.[14] As a framework for the individual stories the cycle has the advantage that is suggests a broad frame of reference going far beyond the individual story and even far beyond the sum of all the stories that go into it. The effect is of something held in reserve—many unsung heroes, many untold tales.

Babel tends to see the world schematically. More important than the features that distinguish one man from another, one landscape from another, are those features that connect men and landscapes with other men and landscapes in the author's memory or the book's accumulation. In *Red Cavalry* the connection between such heroes as Savitski, Pavlichenko, and Diakov is immediately apparent to the reader. The heroes are linked by details of description such as the flamboyant dress they all affect, by the nature of their approach to the world, and by similarities in the structure of the stories.

The majority of Babel's stories fall into three cycles, the

[14] In 1932, Babel added the story "Argamak" to *Red Cavalry*. In 1937 he published "The Kiss," which undoubtedly would have been added to *Red Cavalry* had another edition been published during the author's lifetime. The Czech translator of *Red Cavalry* has followed what he takes to be Babel's intention in including this story in the cycle.

Odessa stories, *Red Cavalry*, and the stories of childhood and coming of age. There are other fragmentary cycles in the body of work such as a series that was to be called "From a Petersburg diary," of which the only complete story to survive is "The Road" ("Doroga"). The Babelian cycle is, like the epic cycle, a series of stories united in the experience of a single individual, but it is more than this. Each cycle also has its style, its particular voice, and each cycle is devoted to a mode of exploration of Babel's common themes of justice and art. In the Odessa stories the tone is comic irony and the mode is heroic. *Red Cavalry* is a more complicated cycle held together by the tension between opposites, between the *intelligent* and the Cossack, between comic irony and profound meditation. The childhood stories are united by their tone of wise contemplation and by their theme of the attainment of knowledge.

The cycle as a form is something more than a series of stories and something less than a novel. In the novel the elementary structure is A leads to B leads to C. In the cycle (if it is more than a mere stringing together of a number of stories) the elementary structure is A equals B equals C. The separate episodes have a weight that is determined outside their places in the cycle, by their own qualities and interest. The episodes determine the cycle rather than the cycle the episodes. *Red Cavalry*, the cycle of Babel's work that most closely approaches the form of the novel, differs from the novel in that the significant unit of structure is the story. The narrator of *Red Cavalry* will never come to understand more than he understands at the end of the first story, "Crossing the Zbruch," although the revelation he experiences there will recur in other circumstances, its relevance to other situations will be demonstrated, and the reader's sense of the meaning of that revelation will be refined and sharpened by repetition.

The result is that one cannot refer to the details of the stories of the cycles out of context as one might in a study of a novel. The meaning of details is circumscribed by the story in which they appear. It is the stories themselves that are comparable units in the cycle. This difference is clear if we consider inconsistencies within the cycle that Babel made no effort to correct. In the story "The King," Benia Krik is wed to the daughter of the rich dairyman Eikhbaum, but in another story of the cycle, "The Father," he becomes betrothed to Froim Grach's daughter Basia. Such "forgetfulness" would be unforgivable if it occurred in a novel, but liberties of this kind are possible in the cycle, where the demands of the story come first.

The cycles are spatial as the stories are spatial. They do not unfold in time but are indeed cyclical, returning again and again to the same point. We trace the general pattern over and over. Each story is a new game with a new strategy, and it is up to the reader to begin afresh each time if he wishes to play the game. Yet Babel, like his beloved Spinoza, has the desire to seek the whole in the parts, to go back to first principles, to proceed in orderly progression from one stage of proof to the next.[15]

---

[15] Many of Harry A. Wolfson's comments on Spinoza's style in his great study are strikingly applicable to Babel's work: "It [the *Ethics*] uses language not as a means of expression, but as a system of mnemonic symbols. Words do not stand for simple

This habit of mind is elaborated into a style, into a structure. To read a story by Babel properly, one must take cognizance of its geometry. The body of Babel's work can be regarded as a larger geometry in which the problem is stated now in one set of terms and now in another, but always in relation to the larger scheme.

---

ideas but for complicated trains of thought. Arguments are not fully unfolded but merely hinted at by suggestion" (p. 22). "In its concentrated form of exposition and in the baffling allusiveness and ellipticalness of its style, the *Ethics* may be compared to the Talmudic and rabbinic writings upon which Spinoza was brought up" (p. 24). From Wolfson, *The Philosophy of Spinoza* (New York: Meridian Books, 1961).

3. The Search for Style and Form

Babel's first appearances in print are contemporary with the great experiments in literary and artistic modernism of Russia's last years before the Revolution. Babel, a contemporary of the Futurists and the Formalist critics and acquainted with them through the offices of Gorki's *Chronicle*, seems completely untouched in these early works by the experimental work of his contemporaries. There is no "trans-sense language," no playing with the levels of time, no attempt at a musical or "spatial" form. Of course, it is unfair to judge many of these works by the standards of a developed avant-garde literature, for they are sketches dashed off for newspapers. But the stories that Babel published at this time are also quite conventional in form.

More interesting than the form of these works is Babel's emerging attachment to the human situation. The sketch or story takes shape around a clearly defined set of circumstances that Babel exploits for its pathos, humor, or color. Yet with one exception the works are anecdotal, sentimental, and rather thin. They lack that richness of understanding of motive which informs Babel's mature stories. They group themselves into several series, each of which is of some interest to anyone trying to trace Babel's development, but none of much interest to the general reader.

In his autobiography Babel reports that the first works of his adolescence were written in French. None of these manuscripts have survived, nor do we know exactly when he made the transition to Russian or what his earliest Russian works were like. Recently there came to light what appears to be Babel's earliest publication, a story, "Old Shloime," published in the Kiev bimonthly *Flares* in 1913, when Babel was seventeen years old.[1] At this time Babel was studying at the Institute of Financial and Business Studies in Kiev and apparently had established contact with the Jewish literary community in Kiev, perhaps through the Gronfeins.

"Old Shloime" is an attempt at a Jewish "slice of life." Its chief character is an 86-year-old man who is living out his last days in his son's family. His is a minimal life, and all of his energies are absorbed by his obsession with getting his share of food. But when his son decides to convert to the Christian faith to avoid being run out of the village, a drastic change takes place in the old man: his forgotten faith awakens, and he hangs himself in shame over his son's desertion of his people. The story may reflect Babel's experiences working among the poor for a Jewish welfare organization or it may be an exteriorization of his own feelings of guilt about questioning his faith (it was at about this

[1] "Staryi Shloime," *Ogni*, no. 6, 1913, pp. 3–4.

time that he took up Tolstoyanism). It is surprising to find a young man turning to the aged as subject matter. In any case, while perhaps not a bad start for a seventeen-year-old, the story is heavy-handed, excessively sentimental, and melodramatic. It is most interesting for revealing a course rejected by Babel in his later writing: the sentimental treatment of the Jewish problem. When the stereotyped figure of the old Jew appears again in Babel's later work in Tsudechkis, Arye-Leib, and Gedali, the whole tone has undergone a change, the most important change in Babel's development as a mature artist.

The teens was a time for literary manifestoes. Babel had scarcely reached Petersburg when, with youthful bravado, he published a declaration of his own literary principles. He did not choose the form of the manifesto but incorporated his views about literature into a series of sketches that appeared in 1916 and 1917 in the Petersburg publication *Journal of Journals*.[2]

"How well Gogol would have described them!" the

---

[2] "Publichnaia biblioteka," "Deviat'," "Odessa," "Vdokhnovenie," *Zhurnal zhurnalov*, 1916–1917. There is some discrepancy in dating in various sources. I had access to photocopies of the articles, which did not bear the date or place of publication. The sketches and other materials discussed in this chapter have been published in English translation in *You Must Know Everything*. Two of the sketches, "The Public Library" and "The Nine," were republished in *Literaturnaia Rossiia*, March 13, 1964, where the place of original publication is given as *Zhurnal zhurnalov*, 1916, no. 52. These two sketches were subsequently published in the New York émigré newspaper *Novoe russkoe slovo*, March 29, 1964.

author exclaims in the first of the sketches, "The Public Library." Gogol's influence is easy to discern in the sketch, both in Babel's choice of the intentionally prosaic subject and in his method of description: "Even the people who work in the coat room are enigmatically silent, full of meditative peacefulness, neither brunette nor blonde, but something in between." The types who frequent the library are observed with humor. The sketch can be regarded as an exercise in capturing the essential traits of a number of characters.

Another sketch, "The Nine," not only reflects the author's experience as a young writer making the rounds of editors' offices, but also provides a comic catalogue of clichés current in the literature of the day. A young poetess writes, "You want my body. . . . Take it, my enemy, my friend. But where am I to find a dream for my soul?" Another of "the nine" waiting in the editor's anteroom is a "coupletist"—he writes couplets on topical subjects like the war. Another of the literati, the Jew Korb, is writing a play, *The Tsar of Israel,* which begins, "Ring the bells. Judea has perished." All of the works have in common an unfailing tone of gloom.

Two of the sketches are even more clearly statements of an artistic credo. A Soviet scholar has said of "Inspiration": "In this sketch Babel is concerned with the very process and psychology of creativity, with the difficulties and paradoxes that lie along the path to the creation of a work of art." [3] This sketch, unlike the other three, has a plot. A

[3] I. A. Smirin, "Na puti k *Konarmii*" [En Route to *Red Cavalry*], *Literaturnoe nasledstvo,* vol. 74, p. 470.

friend comes to the narrator to read his manuscript. He is in a state of great emotion, full of "inspiration." The story turns out to be trivial and unoriginal: "The words in that story were boring, tired, smooth as polished pieces of wood." The narrator tries to suggest to the writer that there are flaws in the story, but, wishing to avoid hurting him, is forced into offering insincere words of praise. The would-be writer is elated by the praise and tells the narrator of his daydream of going to Petersburg and launching his career. The narrator returns to his home after having escorted the elated dreamer home. "I was very sad," he reports.

At one point in the story the narrator observes that there are no corrections on his friend's manuscript. Babel rejects the popular idea that works of literature are the product of inspiration. The story suggests that masterpieces are not written at a single sitting, in a burst of inspiration, but require long, hard work. It is also interesting how much Babel is concerned with the importance of words here, with freshness of language. He is committed at the beginning of his career to those standards of craftsmanship that will later astonish his contemporaries.

Another sketch, "Odessa," is more concerned with tone and choice of subject than with craftsmanship. Here, Babel makes that opposition between Petersburg and Odessa which was to become important in his later work. According to Babel, the Petersburg tradition produced a literature which lacks

a really joyful, clear description of the sun. Turgenev sang dewy mornings and the calm of night. In

> Dostoevsky, one senses the uneven and gray road along which Karamazov goes to the tavern. These gray roads and veils of fog smothered people. Having smothered people, [the writers] gaily and terribly tortured them. They gave birth to the smoke and stink of passions. They made people toss about in the usual human torments.

Babel praises Gogol's "little Russian" stories, in particular "Taras Bulba," and regrets that Gogol turned away from his early romanticism to the gloom of Petersburg.

Babel goes on to say: "Gorki was the first person to speak in a Russian book about the sun, to speak with exaltation and passion. He loves the sun because in Russia things are rotten and twisted, because in Nizhny and in Pskov and in Kazan, people are unstable and dull—are either incomprehensible or touching or boundlessly and stupefyingly boring." In spite of Gorki's romanticism, Babel feels that Gorki is not the ideal which he seeks. Gorki is "not the singer of the sun, but the oracle of truth." Therefore, he is only a forerunner. What Russia needs, Babel assures us, is a Maupassant. Gorki "knows why he loves the sun, why he should love it." But "Maupassant knows nothing, or perhaps he knows everything." Babel prophesies: "We need to refresh our blood. Things are getting stifling. The literary Messiah for whom we have waited so long and so fruitlessly will come from out there—from the sunny steppes washed by the sea." [4]

[4] Babel's prophecy is borne out by the importance of Odessa writers in the literature of the twenties. Many writers not from

Babel's sketch "Odessa" can be taken as his literary manifesto. He calls for an end to dreary concentration on the dark side of life and human nature and a return to optimism and color in art. Babel demonstrates what he means in his description of Odessa, whose chief qualities, he tells us, are lightness and clarity (*legkost' i iasnost'*). His city is peopled by "the muscular, bronze figures of young men who go in for sports, the fat, potbellied and kindly bodies of 'negotiators,' by pimply and emaciated visionaries, inventors and brokers."

Babel outlines a program for himself in the sketches: to follow the example of Gogol in endowing prosaic objects and people with a new vividness through the precise and fresh use of language, to meet the most demanding standards of craftsmanship, and to avoid the gloom characteristic of so much of Russian literature in the past.

Babel's program is not wholly carried out in his first two published stories, which are all too full of the very kind of dreary urban life that he here criticizes. Babel chooses as subject for these stories the pathetic and victimized man, whom we usually call, with appropriate sentimentality, the little fellow. He places his characters in the gray zones of existence between full respectability and criminality or between material comfort and harsh necessity. There is nothing new in his choice of character and situation. From Chekhov on, one line of development in the Russian short story had emphasized the ordinary man and the pathos of

---

Odessa came from "out there"—from the steppes, from the Caucasus, or from Siberia.

everyday life. Many of Gorki's stories belong to this tradition.

The two stories that Babel published in 1916 in Gorki's magazine *The Chronicle* recall the stories of Gorki and Bunin.[5] Both stories share a certain "naturalism" of environment. The first of the two, "Mama, Rimma, and Alla," deals with a family struggling to stay in the ranks of bourgeois respectability. The father is away in Kamchatka, the mother rents out rooms, the apartment is dirty and poorly kept, there are financial difficulties, and the two daughters are pursued by unscrupulous men. The second story, "Ilia Isaakovich and Margarita Prokofievna," is about a Jew who has been caught staying illegally in Orel and spends the night with a prostitute to escape detection.

We hear in these rather grim stories that note of insistent optimism which will later become a chief feature of Babel's work. The central character of the first story is the strong mother who struggles to keep her family together in spite of financial difficulties, the absence of the father, and the daughters' rebellion. During the day in which the story takes place, two of her roomers leave, demanding their rent back; she has a quarrel with a third roomer about his attempts to seduce her daughter Rimma; she goes out to get money from some source to bolster the family finances and returns home in the evening to find Rimma trying to abort Alla, who had given in to her lover and is pregnant. But after these fantastically trying events, she sits down to

[5] *Letopis'*, 1916, no. 11. English translations are available in *The Lonely Years.*

write a letter to her husband that is only mildly complaining, expressing the wish that he would return. We are left with the impression of a simple human being, carrying on against great odds and without any particular talents, but carrying on.

In the second story, the optimism is reinforced by Babel's successful comic creation of the atmosphere of domesticity that develops in the hotel room where the incongruous couple, the Jewish businessman and the Russian prostitute, are spending the night. Ilia Isaakovich openly expresses his belief in the goodness of man. Speaking from her own experience of the world, the prostitute says, "People are bad." But Ilia answers, "No, they're good. They were taught to think they were bad and they believed it." His optimism is vindicated by the friendship that develops between him and the prostitute, Margarita.

Babel's handling of his materials in the two stories hints at the skill of the later stories. The scene in which the mother discovers Rimma aborting Alla looks forward to later climactic scenes in Babel's work. It offers the surprise, the sensationalism, and the neat resolution characteristic of many of Babel's mature stories. In "Ilia Isaakovich and Margarita Prokofievna," Babel uses an incongruous situation for comic effect in a way that reminds us of scenes in the Odessa stories such as the comic duel between little Tsudechkis and Liubka Cossack.

In spite of the skill of the stories, Babel has not circumvented the danger inherent in his choice of subject matter. In the first story, the characters are too slight to bear the weight of catastrophe that the author inflicts upon them. The message of the second story—that a Jew can bring warmth into the life of a simple Russian prostitute—is a bit unsophisticated, and the story is saved only by its flashes of humor. Babel reports in "The Beginning" that Gorki said about his work in this period: "It has become evident, sir, that you understand nothing clearly, but you guess at much." Babel's lack of "understanding" may be seen in his simplistic and sentimental approach to his characters in these two stories.

Nor did Babel escape from the worst temptations of Petersburg in the next series of sketches that he published in the newspaper *New Life* in 1918.[6] (We shall see that he never wholly escaped from that dark view of life which Petersburg symbolized for him.) The gloominess of the sketches from *New Life* is understandable, for they deal with the chaos of the capital in 1918. They are sharp, laconic, striking in effect. The subjects that he seeks out for these sketches are revealing. He goes to the slaughterhouse, to the morgue, to a home for blind veterans, to the jail. These somber excursions are balanced by visits to a home for premature babies and to a former school for orphan girls that has become a maternity ward. The stories reflect both extreme bitterness about present deprivation and abuses, and hope for the birth of a new generation and a new life. In the home for the blind, a girl is undergoing childbirth while her blind husband sits plaiting a basket. The sketch ends on a note of irony: "This child will be, in truth, a child of our times."

[6] *Novaia zhizn'*, 1918. March 3, 13, 16, and 18. May 3 and 6.

As must be obvious from the list of subjects, the emphasis is again on the victim, and in its state of chaos the city provides no end of victims. One of the most effective sketches is entitled "About Horses" ("O loshadiakh"). Babel goes to the slaughterhouse, where he finds not cattle, but horses. From five hundred to six hundred horses are slaughtered a day for food. (There is nothing to feed them anyway.) Babel's love for the striking detail is apparent here. As he goes into the slaughterhouse, he notices the only cattle: the fat bronze oxen that decorate the main gate.

One of the sketches, "Evening," published in May 1918, deserves comparison with Babel's stories. Its structure is complex, consisting of three episodes related to one another only through ironic juxtaposition. The sketch begins with a misleading ironic sentence: "I will not draw conclusions. I am not qualified to do so." The "conclusions" that the narrator refuses to draw are, of course, made by the tale itself, by the juxtaposition of the various parts. Babel describes the brutal arrest of a seventeen-year-old boy who is dehumanized by deprivation, by "well-fed, fleshy people in new boots." The scene of the arrest is juxtaposed with two other scenes. In one episode, the narrator goes into a nearby cafe where music is heard. The sight is dazzling—electric lights, young men in colored uniforms and shining boots, German soldiers. They are vain and self-assured and, above all, calm. In the third episode of the sketch the narrator is in the streets of Petersburg. It is the evening of the title. The first white nights of the year have come. The streets and the Neva are silent and empty. The final paragraph turns to the narrator, to his reaction to the series of events he has witnessed: "The insubstantial veil of night lay over the golden spires. The silence of these wastes hid a thought—easy to understand and merciless."

In the sketch we see Babel tentatively advancing the narrator toward the center of the story. He manages a fullness in the narrator's response to events that is lacking in the characters of the sketch and in their situations. He does not yet dare burlesque the characters or make them larger than life. The boy is a pathetic victim. The police who beat him and the lucky men in the bar are common scoundrels and brutes.

In the *New Life* sketches, the conflicting tendencies in Babel's work come into sharper opposition. The hardships and injustice of life in Petersburg in 1918 bring a new note of bitterness. At the same time, the optimism becomes more insistent. If "Evening" is wholly dark, Babel searches in the other sketches for a sign of hope. He sometimes finds it in the presence of mother and child.

If the *New Life* sketches convey Babel's reaction (in a fragmentary manner) to the Revolution, the next group of sketches published in the Odessa journal *Lava* in 1920 turn to a surprising subject, one already left behind in the Russia of that day, the First World War.[7] Possibly they reflect Babel's first experience of war during his service on the Rumanian front. As a preface to this series, Babel writes: "The stories published here are the beginning of my obser-

[7] "Na pole chesti," "Desertir," "Semeistvo papashi Marescot," "Kvaker," *Lava*, Odessa, 1920, no. 1. I had access to photocopies of these materials.

vations on war. Their subject matter is borrowed from books written by French soldiers and officers, participants in battle. In several passages the plot and form of exposition are changed. In others I have tried to keep close to the text of the original."

The subjects for these sketches, as Babel presently tells us, are drawn from a book by Gaston Vidal.[8] The sketches are even darker in tone than the sketches of Petersburg in 1918. Babel also tries out the laconic description that will be a chief feature of the *Red Cavalry* stories.

The sketches are most important because they show that in the year before Babel joined the First Cavalry in its Polish campaign he was preoccupied with the subject of war and its treatment in fiction.[9] The form of the sketches comes closer to the *Red Cavalry* stories than anything Babel has yet written. Babel's use of another man's materials in the sketches makes it natural for him to introduce two narrators. Many of the sketches have a French officer as primary narrator, but occasionally the author's voice intrudes to call our attention to an irony that is not apparent to the primary narrator. One sketch, "On the Field of Honor," ends: "All that I have told here is the truth. It is related in a book written by Captain Gaston Vidal, *Figures et anecdotes de la grande guerre*. He witnessed this event.

---

[8] *Figures et anecdotes de la grande guerre*, Paris, 1918. Only one of the sketches, "The Quaker," does not take its subject from the Vidal book. A source for this sketch has not been located.

[9] Vidal's book was published in France in 1918, which makes it probable that Babel wrote his series in 1919.

He also defended France, our Captain Vidal." Another sketch, "The Deserter," ends with an ironic reference to the source, Captain Vidal: "Vidal testified that this captain [the one who shoots the deserter] was truly a patriot, a good soldier, a good father and a man who knew how to forgive small injuries. That is not a small thing in a man— to forgive small injuries." Another sketch, "The Family of Papa Marescot," is interesting for its use of the first-person narrative. The narrator, a sensitive, cultivated young officer, makes a good foil for the simple old peasant Marescot, who begs permission to bury his family. (His difficulty, it turns out, is that the officer is sitting in the family grave.)

The *Lava* sketches foreshadow *Red Cavalry* not only in their use of the narrator, but in their anecdotal quality. "The Family of Papa Marescot" has the kind of sharp and ironic climax that will become a chief feature of the *Red Cavalry* stories. Here we also find many of the themes of *Red Cavalry*. In "The Quaker" the chief character anticipates the narrator in *Red Cavalry:* a misfit, a man of peace, a lover of horses. In several of the sketches Babel deals with cowardice and the inability to kill. The *Lava* sketches are the last works that Babel published before he joined the First Cavalry in its Polish campaign in 1920. They may be said to mark a boundary in his life as a writer. When he began to publish again upon his return from the campaign, Babel had found a new voice. The nature of that change and its relationship to the earlier work will be discussed in Chapter 4.

Before we consider the Odessa stories and *Red Cavalry*,

there is one other piece of early work that deserves examination. The sketch "Childhood: With Grandmother," which was published for the first time in a recent volume of the distinguished series *Literary Heritage,* is dated Saratov, 1915.[10] It is curious that Babel did not publish then or later this piece of work so clearly superior to other things he was publishing at the time. The sketch is apparently autobiographical, a description of a typical Saturday spent with his grandmother in her room in the family's apartment. Though the approach is simply descriptive, the organization of the materials shows a high degree of sophistication. The sketch might be included among Babel's childhood stories of the middle 1920's without evoking unflattering comparisons. It differs from these stories only in its leisurely style and in its failure to generalize from the particular case of the characters at hand to the larger world. In the later stories, the experiences of the characters become more abstract and generalized. Here the experience is still specific, though the sketch is organized around a formula, an opposition between two alternatives, in much the same way as the later stories. The "point" of the sketch is expressed in the following passage:

> Grandmother sat unmoving and even the hot, stupefying air did not stir, as though it felt that I was studying and should not be disturbed. It grew

[10] "Detstvo. U babushki," *Literaturnoe nasledstvo,* vol. 74, p. 483. According to the editors of the volume, two pages of the sketch near the end are missing from the manuscript. The last sentence is preserved on a separate sheet.

hotter and hotter in the room. Mimka the dog began to snore. Before that it had been silent, ghostly silent. Not a sound had been heard. Everything was unfamiliar in that instant, and I wanted to run away from everything and at the same time I wanted to stay there forever.

The child is torn between the desire to stay in the shut and locked, warm and secure world of his grandmother's room and the impulse to "get a breath of air," to flee into the exciting world outside.

Babel also opposes the boy's genuine attraction to literature and knowledge to the dead weight of lessons. On this Saturday he has six classes at the gymnasium and returns home to do his homework and take lessons in French, Hebrew, and violin. He finds more burdensome than the lessons his grandmother's inordinate hopes for him, that he will become a *bogatyr*, by which she means a rich man.[11] "Study," she encourages him. "Study and you will attain everything—wealth and glory. You must know everything. Everyone will bow down and be humble before you. Everyone must envy you. Don't believe people. Don't have friends. Don't give people money. Don't give them your

[11] *Bogatyr* is the Russian name for the legendary heroes of Russian heroic songs and tales. The word for wealthy is *bogatyi*. The grandmother, who scarcely knows Russian, confuses the two. A recent émigré from the Soviet Union of Jewish background tells me that her mother used *bogatyr* in this sense and that it is common Jewish usage.

heart." The grandmother tells the boy terse stories in which a harsh justice figures:

> Long ago, many years ago, a Jew had a tavern. He was poor, married and burdened with children. He traded in illegal vodka. A commissioner came to him and made trouble. It became hard for him to live. He went to the saddik and said, "Rabbi, a commissioner is vexing me to death. Plead to God for me." "Go in peace," the saddik said to him. "The commissioner will quiet down." The Jew went away. On the threshold of his tavern he came across the commissioner. He lay dead with a purple, swollen face.

A counterinfluence is exerted on the child by the memory of the grandfather, who "didn't believe in anything except people," who "gave all his money to friends," and who "was governed by an unquenchable thirst for knowledge and for life." This very early work reflects Babel's knowledge of those two opposing views of the world that exerted attractions on him: the grandmother advances the claims of a harsh justice, the grandfather the claims of a generous humanitarianism.

The early work goes off in various directions as Babel tries out subjects and searches for a satisfactory form. Yet no matter what subject he deals with, his eye wanders to the striking detail. Again and again he seizes upon what is moving in the human situation—violence, distress, pathos. It is clear that the weakness of his writing is his tendency to choose the stereotyped character or situation. The characters in the stories fall back—they are stereotypes. The narrator comes forward. Only what is closest to the author, his own reactions to events, emerges strongly and clearly. Perhaps most important in these sketches, he has explored a range of subjects that corresponds to the entire work of his mature period: war, urban life, and the experience of childhood. He has begun to think of his subjects in terms of formulas involving opposites: freedom and security, cowardice and the inability to kill, the gloom of Petersburg and the sunshine of Odessa. A fundamental opposition is already apparent between the pessimism caused by a knowledge of the injustices and deprivations of urban life or war and the optimism produced by his will to find people "good." In short, the characteristics of his future work are present, but they still require a point of view, a form that will bring them together.

Babel later tried to expunge this period entirely from his writing career. He liked to recall only the publication of the two stories in *The Chronicle*, and even they were worth remembering more because of the flattering association with Gorki than because of any merit Babel saw in them. For Babel this work of his youth was a subject for humor, for irony, or, best of all, for silence. Silence became early an important tactic in his dealings with the world.

4. The Victim Becomes Hero: The Odessa Stories

No matter the ugliness and hardship of Babel's world, we come away from it with an impression of its dazzle. Its chief quality is caught for us by Babel in a single phrase: "We looked upon the world as upon a meadow in May traversed by women and horses." It is Babel's delight in the visible world that so animates his stories and that produces much of our pleasure in them. The symbol for Babel of the world's beauty and luxury is his native city, Odessa. From his earliest published sketches his work becomes witty and lyrical when he taps the Odessa vein in his temperament.

Soon after his return from the Polish campaign, Babel began work on a series of comic stories that were to become known as the Odessa stories.[1] The first of these, "The King," appears in the Odessa newspaper *The Sailor* as early as 1921. Konstantin Paustovski in his memoirs, *Story of a Life*, reports seeing the manuscript for another of the series, "Liubka Cossack," in the same year.[2] All of the four stories

[1] A Soviet scholar has recently shown that the Odessa stories precede the *Red Cavalry* stories in date of composition. (L. Livshits, "Materialy k tvorcheskoi biografii I. Babelia," p. 118.)

[2] Konstantin Paustovski, *Povest' o zhizni*, p. 345.

that eventually came to be known as "the Odessa stories" —the two mentioned above and "How It Was Done in Odessa" and "The Father"—had been published by early 1924. Because the Odessa stories were not published in a major periodical until after a number of the *Red Cavalry* stories had appeared, it was generally assumed for many years that *Red Cavalry* was written before the Odessa stories. It is significant that Babel did not write *Red Cavalry* immediately upon his return from the campaign. As we shall see, time put a distance between the events of the campaign as recorded in the diary and their transformation into the stories of *Red Cavalry*. Even more important, in the Odessa stories Babel develops a mature style.

The Odessa stories are strikingly different in style and structure from the early stories and sketches. Here the tone changes to a combination of epic and comic. The subjects have been hinted at in the earlier work. Babel turns to his own traditions, the Jewish tradition and the traditions of Odessa, but he combines the familiar with a new exoticism in language and treatment. His Odessa stories are an almost voluptuous celebration of the city written at a time when the country was gripped by hardship and famine. Odessa has become in the modern Soviet Union an old courtesan who has seen better days, shabby, striving for gentility. Even in the years when Babel was writing the Odessa stories, her glory must have already been in decline. What Babel celebrates is the remembered Odessa of his childhood, the Odessa of the great Opera House which was an outpost of European civilization, Odessa the port city which handled the goods of the world. His Odessa glows in the warm light of nostalgia.

In his choice of subject matter Babel turns from the experience of the war. We may suppose that there is a connection between that experience and his choice of subject matter in the Odessa stories, however. Babel's diary of the Polish campaign is extremely dark and pessimistic in tone. It is not only a record of the usual horrors of war; it is also a record of the poverty, misery, and injustice that he found in the Jewish ghettos wherever he went. In the diary and later in *Red Cavalry* he contrasts the Jews of Poland and Galicia to the Jews of Odessa in much the same way that he had earlier contrasted the urban life of Petersburg to that of Odessa. Upon his return to Odessa, he begins to write a chronicle of the Odessa Jews, showing them as a vital, life-loving brave race, very far removed from the resigned and gloomy Jews he had seen in Poland.[3] Lionel Trilling has described in some detail the divergence of the Odessa Jewish tradition from that of Poland. It is not surprising to find that the wealthy Jews of Odessa lived a different kind of life from the poor Jews of Poland, but as Trilling notes: "As for the lower classes, Babel himself represents them as living freely and heartily. In their ghetto, the Moldavanka, they were far more conditioned by their

[3] Alexander Erlich has called to my attention that this generalization does not apply to the Jews of Warsaw, whom, he recalls, Babel found much like the Jews of Odessa.

economic circumstances than by their religious ties; they were not at all like the poor Jews of the *shtetln*, the little towns of Poland, whom Babel was later to see." [4]

The poor Jews of the Odessa stories—Benia Krik, Froim Grach, little Tsudechkis—refuse to accept their lot passively. Benia comes from the same gray middle world as Babel's earlier characters. His father is the drunken teamster Mendel Krik. By descending into criminality, Benia paradoxically achieves heroism and comes to control his fate. Old Arye-Leib says to the narrator in "How It Was Done in Odessa":

> "Suppose for a moment . . . that you are a tiger, a lion, a cat. You can spend the night with a Russian woman and she will be satisfied with you. You are twenty-five. If rings were attached to heaven and earth, you would seize these rings and draw heaven to earth. But your papa is the teamster Mendel Krik. What does such a papa think about? He thinks about drinking a good glass of vodka, about letting someone have it on the chin, about his horses, and nothing else. You want to live and he makes you die twenty times a day. What would you do in Benia Krik's place? You would do nothing. But he did something. That's why he's the king."

In the Odessa stories Babel manages for the first time to render the victim heroic. He accomplishes this by turning to the formulas of the epic, which he uses half ironically,

[4] Introduction to Isaac Babel's *Collected Stories*, p. 21.

half earnestly. In the first of the stories, "The King," he defines the tone and treatment of character that he will use for the entire cycle.

"The King" tells how Benia Krik marries his ugly sister Dvoira to a bridegroom whom he has bought and how he prevents a police raid on the wedding party by setting fire to the police station. The central subject, the marriage of the hero's sister, is in itself an appropriate point of departure for an epic cycle. As soon as this subject is introduced, the author digresses to recount the story of the hero's marriage, which is at the same time the story of one of his feats. We move from the digression back to the story of Dvoira's wedding, which turns into the story of another of Benia's feats, his triumph over the Odessa police. The story ends with a formula borrowed from the epic. The heroes go to bed after their night of revelry and triumph. In a neat reversal of the epic formula the triumphant Dvoira bears her timid bridegroom off to bed.

The epic treatment of the heroes is combined with a lyrical, evocative treatment of setting, the city of Odessa. Indeed, "The King" is as much a celebration of the abundance of Odessa as it is the story of a hero.

At that wedding they set out for supper turkeys, roast hens, geese, stuffed fish and fish soup in which lemon-yellow lakes shone like mother-of-pearl. Over the heads of the dead geese, flowers swayed like elegant plumes. But does the foaming surf of the Odessa sea cast roast hens upon the shore?

> The noblest of our contraband, everything for which the land is famous from one end to the other, produced on that starry, blue night its devastating, seductive effect.

Yet neither the epic nor the lyric tone is the final determinant of style in the Odessa stories. The reader's first reaction to the stories is laughter. Babel has greatly strengthened those comic elements of his style hinted at in some of the early sketches and in the story "Ilia Isaakovich and Margarita Prokofievna." The comic tone partially depends upon Babel's treatment of a group of gangsters in the epic manner. It also depends upon the undercutting of pretense and convention that lies behind many of Benia's feats.

The Odessa tales are a triumph of style, which is perhaps their greatest significance in the story of Babel's development as a writer. The whimsicality of the early sketches explodes into extravagance, the irony suddenly reverberates with intensity, the sentences become taut. A completely new kind of verbal texture appears, combining a profusion of styles: epic bravado, Yiddish humor, Hebraic solemnity, gangster jargon—all woven together in a seamless whole with an artistry that could not have been predicted from the early work. The comic tension produced by the deliberate confusion of styles recalls Gogol.

The vocabulary of the stories is drawn from many varied sources, and one tends to come away with the impression of a verbal cornucopia. In fact, Babel uses special vocabulary rather sparingly, dropping a few piquant examples into his elegant, tightly controlled sentences like plums into a cake. The dialogue is apt to provide the most examples. The Futurist critic and poet Kruchenykh observed that Babel's characters speak not like illiterate peasants but like "the urban proletariat which is acquainted with newspapers and brochures and even a few books. Therefore, the structure of the phrases is well rounded, but the words and sentences often fall apart or get tangled up." [5] Benia Krik reinterprets the vocabulary of business affairs in his pledge to his future father-in-law: "Ia broshu spetsial'nost', Eikhbaum, i postupliu v vashe delo kompan'onom." ("I'll give up my specialty, Eikhbaum, and go into your business as a partner.") Benia's "specialty" is robbery, and as a business partner he intends to offer Eikhbaum "protection."

Perhaps more important than vocabulary are the arresting figures of speech which stud the narrative with a daring that is almost Futurist: "Sweat, rosy as blood, rosy as the foam from a mad-dog's mouth"; "Reizl, tiny and humpbacked, traditional as a scroll of the Torah, reigned over us"; " 'Try me, Froim,' Benia replied, 'and let's stop smearing porridge on a clean table.' "

But the quality of language that gives the Odessa stories their particular flavor does not lie in Babel's use of a special vocabulary or of extravagant metaphor. It is the constant articulation of the story through the suggestion of shifting

[5] A. Kruchenykh, *Zaumnyi iazyk u Seifulinoi, Vs. Ivanova, Leonova, Babelia, I. Sel'vinskogo, A. Veselogo i dr.* [Trans-Sense Language in Seifulina, V. Ivanov, Leonov, Babel, I. Selvinski, A. Veseli and Others], p. 41.

intonations that gives the style such liveliness and brilliance. Theodor Reik says of Jewish humor: "Jewish jokes in print are, properly speaking, incomplete. They should really be heard and seen. Their communication is not only verbal. The gestures and the facial expressions, the rise and fall of the voice of the story-teller, are essential parts of the telling. Such anecdotes are not only told, but acted." [6] The Formalist critic Tynianov thought that Babel managed to suggest precisely these unprintable aspects of humor: "Every conversational word becomes almost physiologically tangible and forces the reader to enter the story; he acts it." [7]

A passage from the dialogue between Benia and one of the gangsters in "The King" shows how much of the effect resides in the shifting intonation:

> —V uchastok priekhal novyi pristav, velela vam skazat'
> tetia Khana...
> —Ia znal ob etom pozavchera,—otvetil Benia Krik.
> —Dal'she.—
> —Pristab sobral uchastok i skazal uchastky rech'...
> —Novaia metla chisto metet,—otvetil Benia Krik.—
> On khochet oblavy. Dal'she...
> —A kogda byget oblava, vy znaete, Korol'?
> —Ona budet zavtra.
> —Korol, ona budet segodnia.
> —Kto skazal tebe eto, mal'chik?

---

[6] *Jewish Wit* (New York: Gamut Press, 1962), p. 33.
[7] Quoted by Kruchenykh, p. 46.

—Eto skazala tetia Khana. Vy znaete tetiu Khany?
—Ia znaiu tetiu Khany. Dal'she.

"Aunt Hannah told me to tell you that there's a
new police captain down at the station."
"I knew about that day before yesterday," Benia
Krik replied. "Go on."
"The captain called the officers together and made
them a speech. . . ."
"A new broom sweeps clean," Benia Krik replied.
"He wants a round-up. Go on."
"And you know when the round-up will be, King?"
"Tomorrow."
"Today, King."
"Who said so, kid?"
"Aunt Hannah said so. You know Aunt Hannah?"
"I know Aunt Hannah. Go on."

The vocabulary is not startling, but the dialogue has verve
because of the repetition of short phrases with varying intonations. The same shifting intonation characterizes the
body of the narrative. The gangsters' laconic, witty dialogue is displaced by the voice of a homespun philosopher:
"Not according to age were the guests seated at the table.
Foolish old age is no less pitiable than cowardly youth. And
not according to wealth. A heavy purse is lined with tears."
Toward the end of the story a similarly witty shift in intonation occurs when the bravado of Benia's dialogue with
the police inspector gives way to the ironically epic tone

of the story's *kontsovka*, or finale: "And when Benia returned home, they were already extinguishing the lanterns
in the courtyard and dawn was occupying the heavens."

The richness of language in the Odessa stories comes
from the combination of various subjects and styles. Babel
fuses the Jewish tradition with the gangster's tradition and
treats the characters in a style that mixes the epic and lyric
with the comic. Each of these sources of subject matter or
styles of treatment contributes something to the style of
the language. The chief effect, as is often true of a successful combination of styles, is comic.

Yet the Odessa stories are more than extended Jewish
jokes. By treating his characters as legendary heroes, Babel
for the first time escapes the "Petersburg" view of life and
human nature that he rejected in his early program for his
writing. The pathetic little man is still present in the Odessa
stories, but he has either been pushed underground like the
poor clerk Mugenstein in "How It Was Done in Odessa"
or he has undergone a transformation like little Tsudechkis
in "Liubka Cossack." Tsudechkis belongs to the Jewish
tradition of the *schlemihl*, a man who, in Theodor Reik's
characterization, "handles a situation in the worst possible
manner or is dogged by an ill luck that is more or less due
to his own ineptness." [8] Tsudechkis gets into his initial pre-
dicament because the landowner to whom he has sold a
threshing machine leaves Liubka's inn in the middle of the
night without paying his bill. Tsudechkis is held responsible
for paying, but he refuses and Liubka's watchman locks

[8] Reik, p. 41.

him up until the mistress's return. Another characteristic of these unfortunate Jews, according to Reik, is that they are able to wrest victory from defeat. "Perhaps they are ruined by success, but they are rescued by failure." [9] Tsudechkis wins out over Liubka through his wit. At their epic encounter Tsudechkis's weapon is his tongue. The ponderous Liubka is no match for him. He finally conquers her when he manages to wean her child from the breast by trickery. Not only is his debt forgiven; he becomes the new manager at Liubka's inn.[10]

The serious undertones of the stories become more apparent if we remember that Benia, too, is presented to us as a victim who protests against his fate and thereby changes it. The meaning of Benia's protest can be determined by looking at his feats. Like a good Odessa Robin Hood, he robs from the rich to give to the poor, but this is the least important of his services. Most of his efforts are devoted to undercutting the pretensions of the respectable Jewish community. By burning down the police station, he shows up the new police commissioner who had vowed to rid Odessa of the bandits. When the respectable dairy farmer Eikhbaum refuses to pay attention to Benia's "requests" for money, Benia not only forces Eikhbaum to "do business" with him, but winds up marrying his daughter. In "The Father" Benia avenges old Froim Grach. The Kapluns

[9] *Ibid.*, p. 42.

[10] On one occasion Babel tried his hand at a story more directly in the Jewish tradition of the *schlemihl*. See "Shabos-nakhamu" in *Izbrannoe*, 1966.

have refused to marry their son to Froim's daughter Basia, because "our dear departed granddad was a grocer and we have to keep up the family name." In every case, the conventional standards of law and order are called into question and a new conception of justice is suggested, based on the rights of the victim.

The very comic treatment of Benia's acts in these stories makes it possible for the author by sleight of hand to turn Benia into a hero. In the moment when the reader's guard is down, Babel substitutes a new interpretation of justice for the old.

Benia's acts take their meaning from the existence of a community in which a common understanding of justice exists. Within the community, actions are governed by a protocol acknowledged by all. Thus Tartakovski in "How It Was Done in Odessa" answers Benia's letter demanding payment and later bargains with him over a pension for Aunt Pesia. It is the cohesiveness of the Jewish community and the sense of a common victimization that make this possible. Babel allows the theme of the oppression of the Jews to run beneath the surface of the story, subordinate to the theme of justice, but illuminating it at every point. In what seems to be an incidental anecdote at the beginning of the story, Babel makes clear the conditions that unify the Jewish community within the city from Tartakovski to Benia Krik. Arye-Leib tells the comic story of how Tartakovski was "buried with a choir." Underlying the comedy are the grim facts that the event took place during a pogrom and that the "burial" was a subterfuge of the

Jewish bandits, who at the right moment drew forth machine guns from the coffin and let loose at the thugs who were beating up the Jews. The narrator, Arye-Leib, skims lightly over the surface of these events, turning our attention away from Tartakovski's terror at being pursued in the pogrom and to his comic horror over the appearance of the machine guns. "Jew-and-a-Half had not foreseen this. Jew-and-a-Half was scared to death. And what householder would not have been scared in his place?" Yet Arye-Leib at the same time makes the point: to be a Jew is to be a victim and to suffer. "Tartakovski has the soul of a murderer, but he is ours. He came from us. He is our blood. He is our flesh, as though one mama bore us."

Babel reminds us that Benia's bravado is linked to his Jewishness. It is through this connection that the reversal of judgment is made. As Benia says to Joseph's mother, Aunt Pesia:

> "If you need my life, then you can have it, but everyone makes mistakes, even God. A great mistake has occurred, Aunt Pesia. But wasn't it a mistake on God's part to settle the Jews in Russia, so that they suffer as in hell? And what would be wrong with the Jews living in Switzerland, surrounded by first-class lakes, mountain air and real Frenchmen? Everyone makes mistakes, even God."

Benia's view of the unjust nature of the universe makes it proper for him to intervene to right the balance. He corrects first of all the imbalance from which he suffers because of a father who denies him a place in the sun. But his greatness lies in going beyond this, in righting the imbalance favoring the rich over the poor and finally even in helping in some measure to right the cosmic injustice.

Benia's act of protest against an unjust universe takes on a further meaning because of the contrast that Arye-Leib makes between Benia's heroism and the attitude of the primary narrator: " 'Forget for a minute that you have spectacles on your nose and autumn in your heart. Stop kicking up a row at your writing table and stuttering when you're among people. Imagine for a moment that you kick up rows in the squares and stutter on paper. You are a tiger, you are a lion, you are a cat.' " Here emerges the opposition between the man of action capable of taking action to end his victimization and the man who smolders with the "rancor of the dreamer's wrath." In this opposition, which will emerge all the stronger in *Red Cavalry*, the special nature of Benia's heroism is illuminated.

But the great triumph of the Odessa stories is the creation of a style. In the new style he has invented for these stories Babel acknowledges as it were the "artificiality" of the treatment of his themes. The very unrealistic, controlled, invented quality of style is a way of announcing that he has embarked on his own creation of the world. In these stories, Babel begins this progress to understanding by turning to laughter. To laugh at the world is the first step toward objectivity. The comic treatment of acts of violence is made possible by Babel's turning away from the Petersburg myth that had dominated the literature of Russia in the nineteenth century and toward the southern myth of Odessa. This was a signal not to look at hardship and brutality with sentimentality, but to see them through the veil of laughter. This new mode of seeing developed in the Odessa stories for the first time gives them a striking uniformity of style and tone. The new comic mode does not become a substitute for understanding. It is a way of freeing the materials from the binding of an outworn convention so as to be able to press on to a greater understanding.

5. Red Cavalry:
The Search for Understanding

I went through two weeks of utter despair here. That
was because of the ferocious cruelty that never lets up
for a minute and because I clearly understood how un-
fit I am for the business of destruction, how difficult it
is for me to break away from the past—from that
which was bad, perhaps, but that which smelled of
poetry for me as the hive smells of honey. I'm all right
again now. So what—some will make the Revolution
and I, I will sing that which is off to the side, that
which goes deeper. I feel that I can do that and there
will be a place and a time to do it.[1]

So says Babel in a letter written during the campaign in
Poland and preserved between the pages of his diary. This
letter touches us with the anguish of Babel's situation in the
First Cavalry. Yet even in the moment of conflict he ana-
lyzes, judges, determines what his course will be. He iden-
tifies the two bedrock responses that set him apart—his

[1] Quoted by Livshits, "Materialy k tvorcheskoi biografii I.
Babelia," p. 123.

86

hatred of cruelty, his love of the past. His bravery, the bravery of an artist determined to live to tell the tale, is apparent. He sees his responsibility as an artist in terms of understanding. Only understanding of "that which goes deeper" can bring the ferocious cruelty he has witnessed within the bounds of the human, can link the shattering present to the sweet past. Babel's determination is to make this effort of understanding. He ends on a note of affirmation, of confidence in himself and in the future.

We may suppose that Babel did not begin this task immediately upon his return from the First Cavalry, because he was still seeking a means of embodying both the concrete impressions of the campaign, its brutality and misery, and the deeper truth that he thought he could show. In the interim he turned away to the writing of the lighthearted Odessa stories. But underneath the comedy of these stories there is extreme tension, which expresses itself as a feature of the style, in verbal fireworks. Babel had been contemplating a turn from sentimental realism since the publication of his "program" in the *Journal of Journals*, but the Odessa stories were the first fundamental break with the early work. They were something entirely new in Russian literature. They did not make the impact they should have because they were not generally known until the first of the *Red Cavalry* stories had been published (as though Gogol's *Mirgorod* had been published before *Evenings on a Farm near Dikanka*). The Odessa stories are the first product of Babel's First Cavalry experience, of the tension generated and of the problems of understanding raised by his experience there. In them we see the stylistic breakthrough that made *Red Cavalry* possible.

In February 1923, five sketches from the *Red Cavalry* cycle were published in an Odessa newspaper.[2] These earliest published works from that cycle reveal an uncertainty about the nature of the stories and the direction the cycle is to take. Three of the works are little related to the Odessa cycle. "Grishchuk" does not differ from the early work in the treatment of the characters as pathetic figures and in the imposition of an artificially optimistic ending upon the story. "Discourse on the Tachanka" and "The Cemetery at Kozin" look back to the newspaper sketches. They are lyrical evocations, poems in prose, that might have become part of a nonfictional, impressionistic account of the campaign.

Published in the same month, indeed before the three slight sketches just mentioned, are two stories that have the true *Red Cavalry* look.[3] These stories, "A Letter" and "The Church at Novograd," take up the two problems of understanding mentioned in Babel's letter, ferocious cruelty and the break with the past. Both stories may be seen as developing out of the bravura style of the Odessa stories.

"The Letter" makes use of the *skaz* style of narrative that had been tried out by Babel in "How It Was Done in Odessa," but now the language of the narration is more akin

---

[2] *Izvestiia Odesskogo gublizpolkoma* [News of the Odessa Regional Executive Committee]. For the first dates of publication of Babel's works, see notes to *Izbrannoe*, 1966.

[3] In *Izvestiia Odesskogo gublizpolkoma* on Feb. 11 and 18, 1923.

to the gangsters' dialogue of the Odessa stories than to the narration of wise Arye-Leib. The story is thematically linked with the earlier cycle in its recounting of the attempt of a family of sons to achieve liberation from an oppressive father. But while the explanation and justification of Benia's acts can be made by old Arye-Leib out of a shared consciousness of oppression and the need for justice, in "A Letter" that justification comes from the actors themselves. Young Kurdiukov, who relates in a letter to his mother how his father and brothers are occupied in destroying each other, reports the words of his older brother Simon, which gives us insight into the reasons for the conflict. The sons and the father find themselves on opposite sides in the Civil War, but this is not the cause of the conflict. On the contrary, the sons have chosen the side of the Revolution because they connect its battle against oppression with the specific oppression they have experienced at the hands of their father.

Simon Kurdiukov's murder of his father cannot be separated from the context in which Babel places it: the father has declared, "I'll wipe out my seed for the sake of justice," and he has already killed one of the brothers and nearly killed Vassily, before he managed to escape. Babel gives legitimacy to the intertwining of the private and public goals by making the old man a policeman under the tsarist regime, a public oppressor as well as a private one. The cruelty that the Kurdiukovs demonstrate toward each other is thus seen to be the result of far-reaching private and public pressures. Babel turns his dismay away from the cruelty of the acts toward the insensitivity of young Kurdiukov, who reports the ferocities of father to son and son to father with seeming indifference. It is not Simon, who acts by his strict code of justice, who seems depraved, but young Vassily, who is unmoved by fear or compassion. The acts of cruelty are placed at a double distance from the reader, being told by an observer (Vassily Kurdiukov) to the primary narrator. Vassily's indifference becomes a strategy whereby Babel can present acts of cruelty without having to fall back upon conventional responses. This is Babel's way of beginning to examine these acts to find "that which goes deeper."

In the second of the stories, "The Church at Novograd," Babel makes use of the literary tradition of Gothic in much the same way that he makes use of the epic tradition in the Odessa stories.[4] Here he deals with his attachment to the past, exorcising that attachment by showing it through the distorting lens of Gothic. Gothic is an ambiguous way of viewing the past, combining horror and fascination. The narrator has a womanish, comic horror of Catholicism and of the old church at Novograd as a symbol of its rich but unsavory past. Indeed, he is very much like that other innocent fascinated by Gothic, Jane Austen's Catherine Morland in *Northanger Abbey*. At the same time the old church and the way of life that has grown up around it exercise a

---

[4] Victor Terras applies the term "travesty" to Babel's use of literary conventions, defining it as "replacing (or distorting) the form of an original without, however, changing the content" ("Line and Color: The Structure of I. Babel's Short Stories in *Red Cavalry*," p. 142).

sensual power over him: "I drank rum with [the priest's assistant]. The breath of an invisible order gleamed under the ruins of the priest's home, and its ingratiating seductiveness rendered me helpless." The narrator is the virginal victim of time. Babel deals with that dangerous feeling the past ("which smelled of poetry for me as the hive smells of honey") inspires by displacing the emotional charge onto the excesses of the Gothic literary style. The reader senses the unease, but the overearnestness of self-examination is avoided. The present triumphs over the past in a burst of masculine energy as the Cossacks become the violators of the church, forcing it to yield up its secrets. The revelation of fraud behind the sumptuous exterior peels seductiveness away from the church for the narrator, who loses interest at the very moment that his wild surmise is confirmed. " 'Away,' I said to myself, 'away from these winking madonnas, deceived by soldiers.' " Thus Babel finds a stylistic equivalent for the formula that lies behind the story: the past is seductive, but it is bad and must be rejected. The story does justice to the narrator's ambiguous feelings while asserting the truth of the formula. Hence the double-edged quality of the story. It acknowledges the difficulties of accepting the formula at the very time it affirms the formula.

"A Letter" and "The Church at Novograd" represent the two basic forms out of which the *Red Cavalry* stories will grow: *skaz*, in which a secondary narrator recounts his story to the primary narrator, and the more lyrically organized structure where the unifying element is the developing understanding or changing stance of the primary narrator.

That Babel was thinking of a unified work and not of individual stories is made clear in a letter which he wrote at this time: "I have published for money in the local *Izvestiia* several disgusting excerpts, disgusting simply because they are excerpts." [5]

Three questions concerning the nature of violence are implicit in Babel's diary of the Polish campaign: What causes men to commit acts of violence? Why do the violated submit? Where should I stand? In *Red Cavalry* he sets the three questions together, as though by seeing them all at once he will be better able to get the answer to each. As *Red Cavalry* took shape in 1923, three kinds of characters emerged, reflecting the three-sided nature of Babel's quest. Most of the stories are centered in the Cossack hero ("The Remount Officer," "A Letter," "Salt" and "Prishchepa") or in the experience of the author-narrator ("The Church at Novograd," "The Road to Brody," and "The Death of Dolgushov"), but by the end of the year Babel had published a story centered in a figure who is distinguished from both narrator and Cossacks, Pan Apolek. In 1924 he wrote to his editor at the State Publishing House, Dmitri Furmanov, "I am still correcting the manuscript. Besides the wild Cossacks, common mortals have appeared. I am glad." [6] In "Pan Apolek," Babel states explicitly for the first time what the nature of his deeper understanding will

[5] Quoted by Livshits, p. 120.

[6] Quoted by L. K. Kuvanova, "Furmanov i Babel," *Literaturnoe nasledstvo*, vol. 74, p. 506. The passage quoted makes it clear that Babel in 1924 was still engaged not only in "correcting" but in conceiving and writing stories for *Red Cavalry*.

be, that it will involve the forswearing of hatred and re-
crimination.

The search for a deeper understanding leads Babel first
of all to examine the men who commit acts of violence, to
examine the problem that caused him to write in his diary:
"Budenny's army brings Communism. A woman is crying."
Babel's diary of the campaign presents two aspects of the
Cossack. He poses the question "What is our Cossack?" and
provides the answer: "Layers: worthlessness, daring, professionalism, revolutionary spirit, bestial cruelty." Again he
writes, "A picture of battle, the cavalrymen return, dusty,
sweaty, red, not a trace of emotion, they killed, they are
professionals; belief in themselves, difficult work." It is the
professionalism of these men that is most alien and appalling
to Babel. They are men whose business it is to kill and
destroy. At the same time, they are awesome figures: "The
Commander of the Division Timoshenko at the staff. A
colorful figure. A colossus, red trousers, part leather, a red
cap, well built, came up from the ranks, was a machine-
gunner, lieutenant of artillery in the past. Legendary
tales." [7] In their cruelty and in their strength the Cossacks
remain opaque to Babel. His understanding cannot come
from observation, but must be arrived at more obliquely.

Babel is helped in his answering of the first question,
"Why do men commit acts of violence?" by the troubling
presence in his mind of the second question, "Why do the
violated submit?" Babel chose to open *Red Cavalry* with a

[7] *Literaturnoe nasledstvo*, vol. 74, p. 498. Timoshenko is the model
for Savitski in "My First Goose" and "Story of a Horse."

story that explores the response of the violated and that indicates the point of departure for his own search for understanding, "Crossing the Zbruch." [8] He dramatizes in this story his own questioning attitude toward the passivity of the victim, expressed in an entry in his diary: "Galicians on the roads, in Austrian uniforms, barefoot, with pipes. In their faces what a mystery of the insignificance, of the commonplaceness of submission." [9] The narrator of "Crossing the Zbruch" comes among the poor Jews with whom he is quartered as conqueror, not bothering to disguise the disdain he feels for their weakness. "Clean this up," he says to the pathetic, pregnant Jewish woman. "How filthily you live." These people seem grotesque and inhuman to him. As two Jews get up to obey his command, they "hop about in silence, monkey-like. Like Japs in the circus, their necks swell and twist." He experiences the same feeling of initial estrangement as he will later experience before the grotesque figures of the bellringer and his wife in "St. Valentine's Church."

The first hint of internal contradiction in the narrator comes in his dream: "I dream of the Commander of the VI Division. He is pursuing the Brigade Commander on a heavy stallion and shoots two bullets into his eyes. The bullets pierce the Brigade Commander's head and both of his eyes fall to the ground. 'Why did you turn back the

[8] The arrangement of stories in *Red Cavalry* is Babel's own. See his letter to Furmanov of Feb. 4, 1926: "I am sending you *Red Cavalry* in corrected form. I reordered the chapters and changed the titles of several stories." (Kuvanova, p. 150.)

[9] Quoted by Livshits, p. 114.

brigade?' Savitski, Commander of the VI Division, shouts to the wounded man—And here I wake up." The dream is an admission of fear, and it draws the narrator close to the fearful Jews he finds himself among. He wakes up to the truth of their situation. He sees what he had been incapable of seeing before, that the old Jew with whom he is bedded down is not sleeping, but dead. He now sees that their fear comes from a very real terror. But Babel takes a step beyond the sympathetic identification of the narrator's fear with the Jews' fear, and this further step is crucial for the whole problem of understanding in *Red Cavalry*. The true meaning of the situation comes not from events but from the way the events were seen by those who participated in them. The Jewish woman now tells him how her father was murdered by the Poles, but in her story her father's submission takes on a new coloring. "The Poles cut his throat as he begged them: 'Kill me in the yard so my daughter won't see how I die.' But they did as they wanted. He died in this room thinking of me." His submission to death acquires a larger humanity, even a kind of heroism, through his selfless concern in his last moments for his daughter. Beyond that the daughter acquires a dignity she did not possess before, for though having no choice but to submit to the fact of her father's death, she does not submit emotionally. She declares her humanity in her cry: " 'And now I want to know,' the woman said suddenly with terrible strength, 'I want to know, where on earth you will find such a father as my father.' " It is the absence of violence in the submissive man that troubles; it troubles because it suggests the lack of an essential vitality. The woman shows in the "terrible strength" of her cry the vitality of her own life force. If violence might be permitted in the violated as a means of declaring his humanity, then perhaps it has the same explanation in the violator. So Babel begins by showing the perpetrators of violence as they might see themselves. He leaves aside the question, "Where should I stand?" and allows the characters to speak for themselves or as he imagines they might speak for themselves had they the deeper understanding to grasp the tie between their actions and their conception of themselves as men.

The leap of the imagination that Babel was required to make to bring the violent Cossacks within the bounds of his newly defined humanity is clear in his treatment of the character of Prishchepa. In entries in the diary about Prishchepa, Babel describes him arguing ignorantly with a Jewish boy about religion, forcing the local population to dig potatoes on a holy day, and attempting to rape a Jewish girl.[10] Yet in the one story devoted to Prishchepa in *Red Cavalry*, he is treated as an epic hero in an episode that "might easily be an incident in an Irish or Icelandic saga and impresses us as the terrible incidents in these do, without taking from our feeling of the common humanity we share with their authors."[11] The great feat of the imagination

[10] *Literaturnoe nasledstvo*, vol. 74, p. 499.
[11] Frank O'Connor, *The Lonely Voice*, p. 369. It is ironic that this story pleases Frank O'Connor so much, for its creation is the prototype of that process of accommodation to violence which O'Connor finds objectionable in other stories by Babel. But of

that Babel performs in *Red Cavalry* is to bring Prishchepa and "common mortals" like Gedali together within the common humanity.

The characters of *Red Cavalry* have in common the ability to protest. The protest may be treated ironically or seriously, but it is always present. It may be the verbal protest of Gedali, Khlebnikov, or the Jewish woman in "Crossing the Zbruch." It may be embodied in a work of art, as in Apolek's paintings, which protest against the denigration of mankind; or in Sashka Khristos's songs, which protest against the injustice inherent in the universe. It may be embodied in an act of violence like the narrator's killing of the goose in "My First Goose" or Matthew Pavlichenko's killing of his master. The characters of *Red Cavalry* have in common with Benia Krik their refusal to submit to their fates, as did Babel's driver Grishchuk, with "eternal silence, boundless inertia." They speak or act.

The many-sided nature of Babel's effort to understand is apparent in the structure of the cycle. The articulation of *Red Cavalry* as a cycle is comparable to the structure of a Babel story. A variety of tones are artfully alternated. Babel avoids drawing together the stories on similar characters and themes and, indeed, carefully avoids any appearance of narrative sequence. Thus, "My First Goose" is placed between "Gedali" and "The Rabbi," breaking into the direct narrative sequence of those two stories.

---

course O'Connor could not know what the real Prishchepa was like or what an effort of the imagination was required to render him heroic.

The *Red Cavalry* stories, as they first began to appear in journals, were given the appearance of segments from a diary—a form that Babel frequently favored. Many of the stories carried a place and time from the campaign in 1920, a detail that gave rise to the notion that the stories were composed on the field of battle. To us, it is clear that Babel writing in 1923–1925 intended to indicate a time and place for the action of the story. These datings suggest the possibility of a chronological sequence following the course of the campaign, and indeed that may have been Babel's original intention, but it was not followed in the final arrangement of *Red Cavalry*. Many of the stories were given no dates, even in the first publication in journals. When *Red Cavalry* came out as a book, dates were removed from some stories ("A Letter," "Italian Sunshine," "Gedali," and others), though in other cases the dates were allowed to remain. All of this suggests some uncertainty on Babel's part as to the role the diary form was to play in the organization of the cycle.

The arrangement of stories in *Red Cavalry* finally ignores to a large extent the dating of individual sketches. The chronological sequence is not followed. We begin in July 1920, go to an undated story, then to a story originally dated June 1920 from which the date has been removed. The influence of chronology is dimly apparent in the overall structure, since the earlier stories tend to be dated June or July while the stories at the end of the cycle are dated August or September. But except for this very general tendency the chronology of events is scrambled. Babel's decision to avoid an exact chronological sequence increases the sense of "spatiality" in the cycle, an impression that is further strengthened by the careful alternation of stories in different styles and on different themes.

The tension underlying the creation of *Red Cavalry* expresses itself in the proliferation of styles. *Red Cavalry* is the most various and complicated of Babel's cycles of stories. He begins with the heightened, brilliant style of the Odessa stories but rings constant changes on it. In "The Life Story of Matthew Pavlichenko" he makes ironic use of pastoral. Matthew is presented as the happy shepherd down to the conceit of his pipes, but Babel contrasts the genuine, earthy sensuality of the peasants with the elegant languor of the convention and shows the brutalization and exploitation of the real cowherd as opposed to the happy innocence of the conventional figure. Indeed, Matthew gradually emerges from behind the pastoral convention, threatening, terrible in his wrath, refusing to be contained by the boundaries of the convention. In "Sashka Khristos," Babel uses elements of the folk story for this most folk-inspired of his heroes. Thus Sashka's mother reports the death of her children to her husband in the riddle form of the Slavic folk tale: "Our children left the yard—our children left the yard feet first." ("Ushli deti so dvora—ushli nashi detki nogami vpered.") In "A Letter," Babel frames the problem of violence in terms of a most conventional literary subject, the struggle of sons against father, as though by doing so to give himself a handle on the resisting materials of his experience. The insight of the Odessa stories

99

that style in itself can be a perfect method for seeing things is developed in *Red Cavalry*, where the uncertainties of Babel's view find their reflection in the constant shifting of the manner of presentation.

The comedy of the Odessa stories is adapted to the new materials. In many stories from *Red Cavalry* we hear a note of horror behind the calculatedly comic surface. Theodor Reik has pointed out this potentiality in Jewish humor. "In the best examples of this kind of humor there is behind the comic façade not only something serious, which is present in the wit of other nations, too, but sheer horror." [12] Reik explains that in such humor, "the emotional charge is transferred from the tragic to the comic." Babel displaces the tension of his response to cruelty and destruction into comedy. But because of the greater seriousness of his involvement in *Red Cavalry*, the serious implications of the characters' situation are easier to see than in the Odessa stories. In "My First Goose" it is extremely funny that the narrator "proves" himself by killing a goose instead of by raping a woman, as the quartermaster had suggested, but the presence in the story of the rejected alternative gives an edge to the comedy. "Salt" and "The Life Story of Matthew Pavlichenko" preserve a comic tone only because the author puts the narration into the mouths of the chief actors and thereby directs our attention from the brutal act to its justification in the mind of the actor.

In this feat many of the difficulties of the acceptance of violence and destruction were resolved. There is no doubt

[12] Theodor Reik, *Jewish Wit*, p. 27.

that Babel was drawn to violence as he was drawn to any display of vitality, perceiving as he did that for some men the divine fire that makes men akin to gods expresses itself only as violence. At the same time Babel loathed violence, because in its other face violence is cruelty. The chief force that drives Babel to explain acts of violence, and by doing so to bring the violators within the code of human behavior, is his intense desire for reconciliation. Babel's insight into violence is that to the violator his act appears just. He faces the difficulty that no reconciliation can occur as long as a single member of the society feels himself outraged by injustice. (In this maximalism we see that side of him which was attracted to Tolstoyanism in his youth.) Yet to avenge injustice creates further injustice. So the emphasis of the work is turned away from resolution of the problem, which must seem irresolvable, to understanding, to discovering what the just claims of each kind of man might be and to examining the ways in which he acts to attain justice. Babel finds a mode of reconciliation in understanding, for when examined at their deepest level the actions of all men derive from a common need. It is in his need for justice that man finds his humanity. The true criminal act is to try to dissociate oneself from humanity by laying claims to a superior virtue, by judging and condemning those whose expression of the common need takes an alien form. Thus we return to the third question, the dilemma of the narrator. This is the course of logic that leads to the narrator's vow, at the beginning of "Pan Apolek," to sacrifice "the sweetness of the dreamer's wrath, the bitter disdain for the curs and swine of mankind, the flame of silent and intoxicating revenge."

The abstract resolution of the problem of violence continually runs into difficulties with Babel's artist's sense of the concrete realities of experience. This sense of experience is most strongly present in the weight of the past, in memory, and in those aspects of the present that pluck the strings of memory with Proustian exactitude. In the stories of *Red Cavalry* the narrator is shown experiencing the weight of the past in various modes. In "The Church at Novograd" the Catholic past symbolized by the church is alien to the narrator, though seductive. The break with it can be treated farcically, for we are not aware of any particular cost to the narrator beyond his surrender of his naive fantasies. In other stories the tone is elegiac. It speaks of acceptance with fond regret. Thus in "Berestechko" the gentle tones of the hundred-year-old letter languish in the narrator's interior ear as he hears the harsh bark of the Commissar in the street below.

The tension between the demands of the new understanding and the claims of the past becomes most severe at the point where the past comes closest to Babel, in the Jewish tradition. Babel projects into the stories of *Red Cavalry* facets of his own identity, his status as an intellectual and as an artist, his Jewishness, even his spectacles. The Jewish tradition becomes the most important aspect of the past with which Babel's narrator must find accommodation.

It is Babel's great significance in the history of Jewish literature in Russia that he was able to see the conflicts of his Jewish characters in universal terms. By the time of the Revolution a very rich Jewish literature had developed in Russia, but it was still a literature confined to the Jewish community.[13] Babel broke through the language barrier by writing in Russian and through the psychological barrier by relating the Jewish problem of identity to more uni versal concerns.

Babel explores the connection between Jewish past and revolutionary present in three linked stories that come nearer to providing a continuous narrative than do any other group of stories in *Red Cavalry*. They do not follow one another in Babel's arrangement, but taken together, "Gedali," "The Rabbi," and "The Rabbi's Son" form a kind of secret key inserted into the structure of the cycle. They place the narrator in the position of judge, in contrast to the stories about Cossacks, which often put him in the position of judged. They trace the narrator's vacillations. To Gedali he takes the harsh tone of justice of the Revolution: "The Revolution cannot help but shoot, Gedali . . . because she is the Revolution." But he ends by accepting at least implicitly Gedali's representation of Jewishness when he asks, "Gedali, today is Friday, and evening has come. Where can I get a Jewish cake, a Jewish glass of tea and some of that pensioned-off god in a glass of tea?"

"The Rabbi" takes up where Gedali left off, but immediately there is a modulation of tone. If Gedali's shop was filled with objects of the past, dead objects, at least they were worth cherishing as evidence of the kindness and

[13] For a description of this literature see Gorelik, *Siluety evreiskikh pisatelei* [Silhouettes of Jewish Writers], Berlin, 1923.

curiosity of Gedali's mind. At the rabbi's the past loses all glamor and becomes threatening. The narrator sees the rabbi's son Ilia, "a youth with the face of Spinoza, with Spinoza's powerful brow, the wan face of a nun. He smoked and trembled, like a runaway who had been brought back to prison after the chase." The narrator understands the evil omen of Ilia's face to mean that the Jewish past cannot serve the young. He rises and goes back to the glamor of the propaganda train where he works. Only the third story, "The Rabbi's Son," suggests the possibility for reconciliation between past and present.

What does Ilia, the rabbi's son, represent to the narrator? First of all, a fellow Jew. But he is a special kind of Jew. Unlike Gedali and his father, Rabbi Motale, Ilia has chosen to cast his fortunes with the Revolution. This puts him on the narrator's side. The things that the narrator finds in Ilia's trunk explain exactly what Ilia is: there are mandates of the propagandist and notebooks of the Jewish poet. This is exactly what Babel's little trunk contained, since he was a political worker and since he was keeping those notebooks that became the basic material for *Red Cavalry*. Thus the contents of Ilia's trunk form a link not merely with the narrator but with the author himself. There are also portraits of Lenin and Maimonides. The narrator directly connects these belongings with his own person: "In a sad and meager rain they fell upon me—pages from the 'Song of Songs' and revolver cartridges."

Like the narrator, Ilia is a Jew who has renounced his tradition to take up an active role in the Revolution. Like the narrator also, Ilia finds some parts of his Jewish tradition too valuable to give up. It is intellectual vigor that links him with his Jewish past—his poet's notebooks and his pictures of Maimonides, ancient Hebrew verse, and pages from the "Song of Songs." The stylized conversation that takes place between the dying Ilia and the narrator compresses a whole history into a few words. He reveals that only his attachment to his mother prevented him from joining the Revolution earlier, but since "when there's a revolution, a mother is an episode," he went to the front at the command of the party organization. In a short paragraph Ilia describes his most heroic feat: "The kulaks opened up the front to the enemy. I took over the reformed regiment, but too late. I didn't have enough artillery." The heroic men of action have failed in their mission. The Cossacks have been defeated. At this point who takes over: the Jewish intellectual upon whom have been grafted the qualities of heroism that were the virtue of the Cossacks. In Ilia we find the author's construction of the perfect man, a man combining the intellectual gifts of the best Jewish tradition with the valor of the Cossacks. Thus does Babel bring together the two chief strands in *Red Cavalry*.

The final paragraph of the story makes clear the narrator's sense of identification with Ilia: "He died before we got to Rovno. He died, the last prince, among his verses, phylacteries and coarse foot-wrappings. We buried him at some forgotten station. And I—who can scarce contain in this ancient body the tempests of my imagination—I received the last breath of my brother." The suggestiveness of the final phrase of the story—"I received the last breath of my brother"—can scarcely be overlooked. The narrator is, so to speak, "inspired" by Ilia; he becomes the inheritor of his gift. And in accepting Ilia as his brother, he makes peace with his Jewish heritage. "The Rabbi's Son" was originally the final story of *Red Cavalry*. It is possible that Babel conceived of it as a conclusion in which all the threads of the work are drawn together—the heroism of the Cossacks, the intellectual and artistic gifts of the passive heroes, and the resolution of the narrator's search.

Yet the rabbi's son is a figure very much like Babel's Cossacks, emblematic, a function of the story's formula rather than a convincing character. *Red Cavalry* puts Babel's wisdom to its severest test. The Odessa scene lent itself to mythologizing. The childhood stories that follow *Red Cavalry* return to an older tradition of confession and self-knowledge. *Red Cavalry* represents a crisis of the author's capacity for understanding. It does not so much give us an understanding arrived at as show the manifold aspects of the examination through which understanding may be reached.

Red Cavalry remains incomplete. Though Babel later added several stories to the cycle, he never attained the full number of fifty stories that he told Furmanov would make up the complete work.[14] Often in later years he expressed dissatisfaction with *Red Cavalry*. It is his most ambitious undertaking, a tantalizing testimony to his brilliance as a writer and to the breadth of his responsiveness as a man.

[14] Kuvanova, p. 506.

6. Red Cavalry: The Hero

Babel's heroes perhaps remain longer in the reader's memory than anything else from the stories. Their importance is reinforced by the anecdotal nature of the work. Henry James observed: "The anecdote consists of something that has oddly happened to someone, and the first of its duties is to point directly to the person whom it so distinguishes." Yet the apparent concentration on characters is misleading, as are so many other aspects of Babel's work. The stories cannot be understood merely by unraveling the psychology of the characters.

The schematic and abstract nature of Babel's thought is very much apparent in his hero figures. They are without psychology. Just as Babel is not concerned to reproduce human speech exactly, neither is he concerned to reproduce full human figures. The hero undergoes no development, nor is the disclosure of his character the chief point of the story. He is a given quantity in the equation, a calculated contribution to the effect of the story. Each hero is a splendid mask representing some quality or cluster of qualities.

The movement of a Babel story takes place in the structure rather than in the characters. This means that the hero figures, while the most appealing of Babel's creations, are actually subordinated to the structure. Their characteristics, their deeds must be such as to lead to the neat and pointed ending. An excellent example of this manipulation occurs in "Grishchuk," a story that Babel never chose to publish in his collected works but that demonstrates several things about his use of his materials.

For this comparison we shall have to rely upon Livshits' account of the notes in the diary. He quotes extensively, so we are not entirely at the mercy of his interpretation of the details found there. In the diary Babel gives this account of his driver Grishchuk, who has been a prisoner of war with the Germans: "Sometimes he bursts out, 'I'm suffering.' He couldn't learn German because his master [a German farmer to whom he has been sent to work] was severe. They only quarreled, but never talked together. One more thing—he nearly starved for seven months because his master was stingy with the food." [1] In the reworked anecdote that Babel published in an Odessa paper, the relationship is considerably changed:

> Grishchuk was taken by a lonely and mentally disturbed farmer. His insanity took the form of silence. By means of beatings and starvation he taught Grishchuk to communicate in sign language. For four years

[1] Livshits, "Materialy k tvorcheskoi biografii I. Babelia," p. 116.

they were silent and lived together peacefully. Grishchuk didn't learn the language because he never heard it. After the German revolution he returned to Russia. His master accompanied him to the edge of the village. They stopped by the highway. The German pointed to the church, to his heart, to the limitless and empty blue horizon. He leaned his gray, rumpled, crazy head against Grishchuk's shoulder. They stood so in silent embrace. And then the German, waving his hands, with rapid, weak, and faltering step ran back to his home.[2]

This transformation reminds us of the sentimentality of Babel's early work, but it is also interesting because the essential natures of both figures are changed. The question which Babel most often asks about Grishchuk in the diary entries—Why doesn't he desert?—isn't introduced into the characterization at all. The most interesting aspect of Grishchuk's psychological makeup is sacrificed to the demands of the story. The German is even more strikingly transformed. His silence, in reality attributable to surliness, is now the result of a kind of divine insanity, the protest of a sensitive soul. And the beatings and hunger that Grishchuk suffers at his hands serve the purpose of teaching and become almost like religious trials that he must undergo in order to

[2] "Grishchuk," *Izvestiia odesskogo gubispolkoma* [News of the Odessa Regional Committee], 1923. Available to this author in photocopy. A brief, factual account of Grishchuk's history, stripped of sentimental speculations, occurs at the beginning of the *Red Cavalry* story "Lecture on the Tachanka."

enter into the divine secret possessed by the insane man. The experience is reordered into a mythical formula. The "truth" that the formula expresses is banal. It lacks the paradoxicality and complexity of the revelations of the mature stories. But in those stories the characters are as much at the mercy of the author's chosen formula as here.

The heroes of Babel's stories are emblematic. His descriptions of them are pictorial, and their attributes are directly known from the description as in allegory. Consider the famous description of Savitski which opens "My First Goose": "Savitski, commander of the sixth division, stood up when he caught sight of me, and I was amazed by the beauty of his gigantic body. He rose and the purple of his riding breeches, his crimson cap tilted to the side, the medals stuck on his chest, cut the hut in half as a standard cuts the sky." The narrator envies "the iron and the flower of that youth," attributes that are more than physical in Savitski. It is these attributes that are of significance for the story, for Savitski stands as a living representation in the narrator's eyes of the Cossack qualities, the lack of which separates him from the community.

The heroes in the cycle are linked by the details of description that become symbolic of certain attributes. It is this constancy in the symbolic use of detail that enables us to perceive an underlying unity in the work. The reader retains not so much a series of individual images of the men as a composite image formed by the representatives of the type. Some individuals, for example the splendid, perfumed Savitski, stand out from the composite type, but even these are more significant for what they contribute to the image than for their distinguishing characteristics. The reader automatically refers to the larger conception in reading the individual story and immediately perceives the correspondence between Pavlichenko, Savitski, Diakov, and so on.

In *Red Cavalry* there are two series of heroes who are linked by symbolic detail and who form two distinct composite types. The type that has always attracted most attention is often thought of as the Cossack type, since a large number of its representatives in the stories are Cossacks. One of the characteristics of this hero is his language—elegant rhetoric combined with incorrect usage. These men speak with one voice, and when they become narrators of their own stories it is difficult to distinguish one from the other. The linguistic peculiarity is a "tag" for certain qualities that are part of the composite picture rather than a means for distinguishing individual speech.

Sometimes the link between heroes is made explicit, as when Nikita Balmashev from "Salt" turns up in the similar story "Treason," or as when Kolesnikov ("The Brigade Commander") is compared to "the famous Kniga, the self-willed Pavlichenko, and the captivating Savitski," all Cossack commanders who appear in other stories. Thus that "masterful indifference of a Tartar Khan" that Kolesnikov shows on the occasion of his promotion is linked with the aplomb shown by other Cossack heroes in their sensational exploits. Often a hero will appear briefly in the context of another story, where his qualities serve to intensify certain aspects of the theme. Pavlichenko appears again in "Berestechko": "Divisional Commander Pavlichenko's felt cloak fluttered over the staff like a somber flag. His downy hood was thrown back over his cloak, and his curved sword lay at his side as if glued there."

The Cossacks ride into the Polish town as the representatives of the new Soviet power, but they are recognized by the townspeople as an older phenomenon—a recurring motif in the history of the Polish-Ukrainian border. "An old man with a *bandura* crawled out from behind a tombstone and in a childish voice sang to us about former Cossack glories." The presence of Pavlichenko at their head recalls without specific reference the Cossack qualities of which he is emblematic.

The most frequent pictorial detail in the description of these heroes is the black cloak that seems to transform them into sinister forces, sometimes even into angels of death. Diakov is introduced as the remount officer "in a black cloak," and as often in Babel this significant detail appears again at the end of the story. "The remount officer . . . swinging his opera cloak, disappeared into the Staff building." The opera cloak is a symbol of Diakov's virtuosity—his tenderness and daring cruelty in dealing with the mare, which he beats and cajoles until the half-dead beast gets to her feet. Pavlichenko's cloak at Berestechko flies above the staff "like a somber flag." At the beginning of "The Death of Dolgushov" an angel of death appears: "At noon there flew past us, wrapped in a black cloak, Korochaev, the disgraced commander of the IV Division, fighting alone, seeking death. . . . He galloped off, fluttering, all black, with pupils like coals."

Not only the pictorial quality but the symbolic value of the black cloak is made clear when it turns up in an unexpected place—a painting by Apolek, the Polish painter of startlingly rich and detailed religious pictures: "The long figure of John the Baptist descended straight upon me out of the blue depths of the niche. A black cloak hung solemnly on that implacable disgustingly emaciated body. Drops of blood shone in the round clasps of the cloak. John's head had been cut off at a slant from the jagged neck."

The reverse side of these heroes, their splendor and beauty, is also pictorially expressed in descriptions of dress. It is not Savitski but his attire that "cuts the hut in half as a standard cuts the sky." Prishchepa wears "a crimson Circassian coat of fine cloth, and a downy hood, thrown back over his shoulders." The heroes appear in costume, arrayed like virtuosi for their parts. Diakov appears not only in the sinister black cloak but in trousers with silver stripes along the sides.

This virtuosity suggested by dress it reinforced by a second set of symbolic details. Many of the heroes are circus entertainers. Diakov is described as a former circus athlete, and at the climax of the story the fascinated spectators form a ring around him in which he performs his trick for their edification: "Straightening his legs, caught at the knee with a small strap, elegant and agile as if on the stage, he went over to the dying animal." Konkin describes himself as "musical clown and drawing-room ventriloquist from the town of Nizhni." Liovka in "The Widow" is a trick rider and weight lifter from Temriuk. In other descriptions where no specific reference to performing is introduced, the glamor and virtuosity of the performer persist as a part of the characterization, for they serve as a metaphorical shorthand for the qualities of the type rather than as a particularizing detail for the individual hero.

These emblematic details turn up in stories outside the *Red Cavalry* cycle, creating a unity that goes beyond the confines of the individual cycles. The Cossack officer in "First Love" shares the splendor of dress of his *Red Cavalry* brethren as well as their disdain for weakness. Babel's most notable hero outside the *Red Cavalry* cycle, Benia Krik, is related to the men of violence by many details of description. His flamboyant dress is worthy of Savitski: "He was dressed in an orange suit, under his cuff gleamed a diamond bracelet." On another occasion he wears "a chocolate jacket, cream trousers, and a crimson vest." Benia's red automobile, with its horn that plays "Laugh, Clown, Laugh," is the equivalent of the Cossack's horse. Benia is, in fact, a motorized urban Cossack. The clue to his place in that constellation is provided in this phrase: "He was passionate, and passion rules the universe."

The second category of heroes are linked together by physical description as much as the first. They are often compared to birds in their fragility and merriment. "Gedali, in his green frock coat, was dozing by the wall like a gaudy little bird." In "Guy de Maupassant," Kazantsev sits dreaming, forever asleep to the reality of the world. "The canary fluff rose on his head." Pan Apolek is associated with imagery relating him to small living things. "From Apolek's thin neck dangled a canary-colored scarf. Three little chocolate-colored feathers swayed on the blind man's [his friend Gottfried's] Tyrolean hat." He is "a combatant roaming the world in a state of blissful intoxication, with two white mice in his bosom and with a set of the finest brushes in his pocket." "Apolek . . . moves about in his corner like some gentle and graceful animal." And Apolek generously offers to include the narrator in his beneficent world by painting him as "Blessed Francis . . . with a bird on his sleeve—a dove or goldfinch, just as the Pan writer wishes."

These heroes are marked by a sign of their physical weakness that is at the same time a sign of their virtue. Apolek is a drunkard, but this weakness becomes a metaphor for his art, his "heretical and intoxicating brush." Apolek's alter ego, the accordionist Gottfried, is blind. It is as if to Apolek had gone the gift of sight, to his friend the gift of hearing: "Bowing his bald head, he listens to the endless music of his blindness and to the whisperings of Apolek, his eternal friend." Gedali is also blind. ("A Pole closed my eyes.") Sashka Khristos is syphilitic, but the disease becomes the sign of his sainthood: "Because of his love and because of his illness, they were never angry with Sashka."

The descriptive details that draw together this series of characters indicate clearly that a certain opposition is set up within the work. If one group of heroes is distinguished by physical splendor, the other is distinguished precisely by physical weakness. This opposition is even more apparent in the characteristic approach to life of each group. The physical man tears away at reality as if trying to strip it down to its basic elements. Matthew Pavlichenko best expresses what might be attained by this approach:

> Then I stomped on my master Nikitinski, I stomped on him for an hour or more and in that time I came to know life in full. With shooting, I would say, you only get rid of a man. Shooting is a pardon for him and vilely easy for yourself. With shooting you never get at the soul, to where it is in a man and how it shows itself. But I, as it happens, don't spare myself, and it sometimes happens that I trample an enemy for an hour or more. I want to get to know what life really is, just what our life's like.

Often the ostensible motive for destruction is revenge, but in every case Babel suggests a more serious goal, the attainment of extraordinary knowledge. Prishchepa, who sets out to revenge the murder of his parents, not only leaves a bloody trail through the village but winds up destroying his own inheritance in a ritualistic frenzy of destruction.

> On the third night the settlement saw smoke over Prishchepa's hut. Torn, scorched, staggering, he led the cow out of the shed, put his revolver in its mouth and fired. The earth smoked beneath him. A blue ring

of flame flew out of the chimney and melted away; in
the stall the young bull that had been left behind
began to bellow. The fire shone as bright as Sunday.
Prishchepa untied his horse, jumped into the saddle,
threw a lock of his hair into the flames, and vanished.

The man of peace, on the other hand, is creative rather
than destructive. He imposes his own vision upon the
harsh facts of reality. This is most obvious in the case of
Apolek the artist, who uses the materials of everyday life,
the faces of common people, but illuminates these materials
with wonderful colors. Gedali has his vision of society, "an
International of good people," and Sashka Khristos dreams
of an existence far removed from the wretched hut of his
parents:

> The ravishing vision conquered him. He gave himself
> up to reverie and rejoiced in his waking dream. It
> seemed to him that two silver bands twisted into a coarse
> thread hung from the sky and to these was attached
> a cradle, a cradle of rosewood all decorated. It swung
> high over the earth and far from the sky and its silver
> bands swayed and shone. Sashka lay in the cradle and
> the air fanned him. The air, loud as music, came from
> the fields, and a rainbow flowered over the unripe
> grain.

Indeed, the man of peace in *Red Cavalry* is characterized
as artist as much as the man of violence is characterized as
performer. Besides Apolek's art, Sashka Khristos has his

singing, and Gedali's criteria for his new society are as much aesthetic as ethical. He feels the injustice of the revolutionaries taking his phonograph as keenly as the injustice of the Poles blinding him.

So the initial conception in *Red Cavalry*, the one first apparent to the reader, is an opposition between the two standards represented by the characters. Yet the individual story remains more important than the cycle, and if we look at the individual story we see that these seemingly opposed types are actually treated identically in the stories.

Many critics have referred to the epic nature of the work. They mean by that partly that Babel adopts some mannerisms of the epic, but chiefly that the characters are treated in the heroic manner. This is true not only of the man of violence whose physical prowess and instinctive bravery easily fit the usual conception of the hero, but also of Pan Apolek, Sashka Khristos, Gedali, and even more unlikely figures. Babel announces his subject in the first story of *Red Cavalry*, "Crossing the Zbruch," where the pathetic and grotesque Jews, familiar figures of sentimental realism, are stunningly transformed into heroes at the end of the story. The stories of *Red Cavalry* are permeated by heroism, the heroism of Trunov, who single-handedly enters into combat with a fighter plane, the heroism of the itinerant painter Apolek, who takes on the Catholic Church, the heroism of the rabbi's son who breaks with his family and traditions to join the Revolution. Whatever the characteristics of the individual figures, it is Babel's custom to show them as exceptional, as men who register their protest in the face of a cruel fate.

Each of his types presents a difficulty to the author who would show his characters in a heroic light. The man of violence is open to the charge of brutality, which neutralizes the glamor of his bravery. Babel solves this problem in *Red Cavalry* by putting the stories in the mouths of the men who act. The most brutal happenings are usually narrated by the men who take part in them. In fact, it is striking that all stories in *Red Cavalry* that are told by a secondary narrator are concerned with acts of violence.[3] The ethical justification in these stories is that of the Cossack who commits the act and not necessarily of the author or even of the primary narrator, but for the purposes of the story justification is provided.

The passive man presents a different problem. He has none of the traditional attributes of heroism, neither physical strength nor beauty. Nor does Babel care to force the irony of the situation by making these men actors in traditional heroic situations. For these heroes he redefines heroism as a moral standard rather than a physical standard. More often than not the passive men demonstrate their virtue after having been defeated by the traditional weapons of power. Pan Apolek and Sashka Khristos possess weapons that are as effective as any Cossack sword or any other instrument of power. The meek Apolek, who would not dream of physical violence, has his own kind of bravery:

> So began an unprecedented war between the powerful body of the Catholic Church on the one hand and the

[3] These are "A Letter," "Italian Sunshine," "The Life Story of Matthew Pavlichenko," "Konkin," "Salt," and "Treason."

carefree painter of holy images on the other. It dragged on for three decades. Chance almost made of the gentle wanderer the founder of a new heresy. And he would have been the most ingenious and entertaining combatant of all those that the Church has known in her devious and stormy history, a combatant roaming the world in a state of blissful intoxication, with two white mice in his bosom and with a set of the finest brushes in his pocket.

Sashka Khristos would seem to be the most passive character of all. He is modeled on the Orthodox ideal of saintliness and is related to Myshkin and all others who desire to live in complete peace with their fellow men and to reconcile all opposites. Instead of opposing his stepfather Tarakanych, he chooses to go away and live alone as a shepherd. But he has a very great power, the power of compassion, and linked to this, the power of his song:

> "Star of the fields," he sang, "star of the fields above my father's house; my mother's grieving hand. . . ."
> And I listened to him, stretched out in the corner on the rotting mattress. Reverie broke my bones, reverie shook the rotting hay beneath me. Through its hot downpour I scarcely could make out the old woman, who propped her faded cheek on her hand.

The language of violence is used here, as in "Crossing the Zbruch," to describe a purely spiritual strength. By transferring the emotional effect to the physical world,

Babel insists upon its reality, thereby making plain his belief in the power of his passive heroes to affect the world.

Babel's types are his own and do not correspond exactly to any particular social group. Babel undermines the reader's natural inclination to associate the types with his own stereotypes. Though the great majority of Cossacks in *Red Cavalry* conform to the type of the man of violence, there are exceptions and not every man of violence is a Cossack. Each type contains a range of characters, all sharing important general features but differing in the emphasis that the author places on one or another aspect of the characterization. Each type is defined by the range of its characteristics as much as by any single characteristic. Many of the Cossacks are described as athletes and performers, but only Diakov is chiefly characterized by this description and only his story depends upon this fact. The same rule applies to moral attributes. All representatives of the passive type possess to some degree the aesthetic view of life, but only Pan Apolek is its perfect representative. In Sashka Khristos the ideal of brotherly love is most fully developed, in Gedali the social ethic. The easy division between Cossacks and Jews, which many critics make in reading the work, is inadequate. In any simple division of the characters, Benia Krik the Jewish bandit must stand with the Cossacks; Pan Apolek, that not-so-good Catholic, and Sashka Khristos, the common man's saint, with Jewish Gedali.

"The Story of a Horse" illustrates how the categories are blurred. Here two Cossacks come into conflict, the earnest

Khlebnikov with the renowned Savitski. Khlebnikov is a curious combination of characteristics. He shares the Cossack love for horses, the anarchical spirit, even the customary bravery. His letter of protest against Savitski's high-handed treatment is couched in the jargon that Babel invented for his men of violence, and his reasoning is based on the Cossack blend of high principles and self-justification. But in spite of these traits Khlebnikov is not the "Cossack" in the story. That appellation is earned by Savitski, who triumphs over Khlebnikov through his cool bravery and self-confidence and who remains the possessor not only of the horse but of the woman. Khlebnikov has the hidden weakness of the aesthetic man, for in the long run his standards are aesthetic. He justifies his claim on the mare that is the object of the conflict by saying that he is "a lover of gray horses." The narrator calls him "a man like me in character" who looks upon the world "as upon a meadow in May traversed by women and horses." Khlebnikov is saved for us as hero by the author's sleight-of-hand when the emphasis in the story is switched from his defeat by Savitski to the letter of protest that reveals his exceptional spirit. But the verbal nature of his protest links him to the passive heroes.

The history of Babel's development as a writer suggests that the chief creative force behind the stories, which not only shapes them but endows them with that curious power over the reader, is the drive to show his characters as heroes. If further evidence is required for the heroic nature of the stories, then we need consider only one overwhelming fact: there are no villains in Babel's stories! When we look for the source of evil in any story (and evil there is in plenty), it recedes into some difficult-to-visualize abstraction, for example "the Poles" in "Crossing the Zbruch" or "the Catholic Church" in "Pan Apolek." In "How It Was Done in Odessa," who can condemn a witty and obliging man like Ruvim Tartakovski, whose well-intentioned letter to Benia went to the wrong address, thereby setting off the chain of events leading to Muginstein's death? In some of the stories there is a curious two-sidedness that cancels out the villainy of both antagonists. In "Matthew Pavlichenko" every reader must sympathize with Matthew's revenge for the many wrongs he suffered, but at the same time sympathy is evoked for the pathetic figure of the old master as he tries to appease his former serf and meets with a horrible death. Here as in many other stories villain suddenly becomes victim, and ready compassion falls around him like a mantle. So each man in turn is shown to be the victim of his fate, and the most despicable acts have a kind of virtue when seen as protests against that fate, as assertions of the human spirit.

But what about the narrator of the stories? Here is a character who is more than a contrived mask of characteristics, a character who reflects, chooses, judges, reacts, who is neither hero nor saint. The generalizations that apply to other characters, however different in appearance, do not apply to him. It is easy to fall back upon that rule of thumb and insist that the narrator is after all not the author.[4] But the truth of the matter is that Babel has not carefully distinguished the narrator from the author, and the stories slide back and forth across the boundary between the two functions.

Perhaps this distinction will be easier to understand if we compare Babel's narrator with two other narrator-characters in literature, Nick Carraway in *The Great Gatsby* and the young man who tells us much of the narrative in *The Possessed*. The reader has no difficulty in distinguishing Nick Carraway from the author and in fixing him as a fictional character in the story, even though the reader assumes that Nick Carraway's attributes and attitudes are very close to the author's own. *The Possessed* presents an even clearer case, for not only is the young man not Dostoevsky, he is clearly looked upon with some condescension by Dostoevsky as a commonplace and limited creature, incapable of understanding the characters he describes. But in *Red Cavalry* there is no barrier of objectivity or irony between the author and the voice of the primary narrator. Readers without exception are persuaded that this is the author speaking directly to them.

I do not mean to suggest that we should assume that Babel is recounting his experience to us exactly as it happened

[4] Some Soviet critics have fallen back upon this cliché in an effort to give a more acceptable reading to *Red Cavalry*. One critic, for example, thinks that Babel takes the same tone toward his narrator as Fadeev takes toward the intellectual Metchik in *The Rout*, that is, he condemns him through irony. (V. Arkhipov, "Uroki," *Neva*, 1958, no. 6.)

to him in 1920 in Eastern Poland. I do suggest that Babel is making use of the appearance of autobiography for effect, that he wants to obscure the line between author and narrator in order to claim the reader's belief. The Odessa stories make very slight use of this autobiographical device, but the childhood stories written later than *Red Cavalry* make extensive use of it. In the childhood stories the narrator is no longer a character at all, but is the author's voice speaking directly to the reader. In *Red Cavalry* the device has not been consistently worked out and the narrator is not clearly character, not clearly author.

The identification of the narrator's voice with the author can account for certain difficulties in understanding the narrator. If an author creates a special identity in his narrator, then he must let the reader know explicitly or implicitly who the narrator is so that the reader can judge the narration accordingly. The author on the other hand is not required to furnish a further definition of himself than the self-evident one. He is "the author of the work," and his whole relationship with the reader depends upon that fact and no other. Insofar as the narrator in *Red Cavalry* speaks in the role of "author of the work," no further information is required nor is it given. But when he enters the story as character, a minimum of information is necessary to the operation of the story. In these cases that very minimum is provided, the one or two facts we need to judge the narrator's actions in the story. What is more confusing, in a single story the narrator may be both author and character.

In *Red Cavalry*, the narrator not only provides the key

125

meaning in the individual stories; he serves as the most important link in the cycle. The *Red Cavalry* stories have two centers of gravity, each exerting a pull on the form of the work.[5] One of these is the hero figure; the other is the narrator, the consciousness through which the story filters to the reader. The stories are not only epic in the sense that they recount the feats of heroes, they are epic in a new and modern sense, one given the word by Stephen Dedalus in *Portrait of the Artist as a Young Man:* the epic, he says, "is the form wherein [the artist] presents his image in relation to himself and to others"; and later, "The simplest epical form is seen emerging out of lyrical literature when the artist prolongs and broods upon himself as the center of an epical event and this form progresses till the center of emotional gravity is equidistant from the artist himself and from others." This is the difference between the figures who are the stuff of the narration in *Red Cavalry* and the consciousness of the narrator. In "Crossing the Zbruch" it is his sudden knowledge that the reader shares at the end of the

[5] In his study of the literature of the 1920's, *Red Virgin Soil*, Robert Maguire sees Liutov, the narrator of *Red Cavalry*, as one representative of a type characteristic of the literature of the times: "These new men are estranged from society and from themselves. They can find no runnels for their moral energies. Although they feel their estrangement acutely, they cannot articulate their anguish, but can only continue to seek its meaning" (p. 327). But, of course, Babel's narrator exists in a much more complex artistic structure than the usual representative of the type. In *Red Cavalry* the earnest examination of the plight of the *intelligent* is under attack by other forces that Babel sets in motion in the stories.

story. Throughout the story we have been limited by his view of things, taking the Jews, as he does, for dirty and disgusting people. The reader can reverse that attitude only because the narrator reverses his attitude. He is the chief controlling instrument in the hands of the author.

Because of the primary importance of the narrator, the other characters, both passive and violent, are seen in relation to him. We find judgments of this sort: "He was a man like me in character." "I was alone among these men." The Cossack has been used again and again in Russian literature as an example of a man who embodies the strength of physique and character so conspicuously lacking in the heroes of Russian stories and novels. When Gogol chose the Cossacks in *Taras Bulba,* he did everything possible to strengthen the mythical nature of his heroes. He went back to the period of the Cossacks' greatest freedom, their heroic age in the seventeenth century. His intention is revealed by the dreamlike quality of his narrative. His Cossacks exist outside time, like the heroes of Arthurian legend. The whole of *Taras Bulba* is a leisurely dream made peculiarly Gogolian by the occasional appearance of those grotesque or startingly trivial details that are the distinguishing mark of his imagination. Tolstoy's Cossacks, on the other hand, are a peculiarly Tolstoyan blend of myth and reality. When Olenin departs for the Caucasus, he expects to find mythical Cossacks like Gogol's heroes, but what he does find is somewhat different. In *The Cossacks,* Tolstoy manages both to *unmask* the myth and to preserve it. The Cossacks are more subject to human weakness and especially less subject to manipulation by Olenin's imagination than were Gogol's heroes subject to his. Nothing better reveals the importance of the Cossack as a dream figure in the Russian imagination than Olenin's expectations. He thinks that they will be, like figures conjured up by our fantasy, subject to his absolute control, ready to become his friend, his mistress, to admire and love him at the command of his will. It is not so much the qualities of the Cossacks that are unmasked. They do indeed turn out to be brave, uninhibited, living freely in nature. But they also turn out to have independent desires and wills of their own, not to be subject to manipulation by Olenin. This is the great discovery Olenin makes, the great disappointment he suffers. The significance of this discovery for him is that he is forever excluded from merging with the myth, from appropriating for himself those qualities he lacks. It is only by remaining in the world of fantasy, as Gogol did, that the illusion of identification with the legendary hero can be preserved. Once the analytical mind begins to examine that illusion, to test it against reality, the illusion must perish. Tolstoy's *The Cossacks* is a book about the destruction of that illusion.

Red Cavalry is not about the destruction of an illusion. But it does include one important element of Tolstoy's examination of the relationship between Russian and Cossack. The narrator of *Red Cavalry* thinks of himself as the opposite of the Cossack. It is the Cossack quality that he lacks and that he longs to appropriate for himself.

Although his sense of difference is not so acute among the passive heroes, the narrator does not fit in there either.

He knows he lacks the perfect grace and compassion of men like Gedali, Apolek, and Sashka Khristos, who understand and accept their lot in life.

The narrator's intermediate position between the two groups of heroes produces a curious discrepancy in his behavior from story to story. His behavior in a given story depends very much upon his *vis-à-vis*. Among the Cossacks he exhibits the weaknesses of the intellectual nonphysical, nonviolent man. He is a man who is unused to the life of violence and hardship in which he finds himself, a man who cannot kill other men, who rides into battle with his weapon unloaded, who cannot even kill a man as an act of mercy. He is timid, apt to panic, not so much for fear that he will be killed as for fear that he will not distinguish himself among the hostile and indifferent Cossacks. Yet when he encounters people whom he judges to be weaker than himself, his tone and behavior change. Suffering from hunger, he takes up arms against his landlady in "The Song." "I smelt meat in her cabbage soup and laid my revolver on the table, but the old woman was stubborn in her denials. A trembling appeared in her face and black fingers, her face grew dark and she looked at me with fright and astonishing hatred." This time the spirit of compassion intervenes to save the situation: "Nothing could have saved her, I'd have compelled her with my revolver, if Sashka Koniaev, called Sashka Khristos, had not prevented me." Sashka lulls the angered narrator by singing and then soothes the old woman by going to bed with her. The story ends with the narrator attempting to think "good thoughts" as he goes to sleep.

In "Crossing the Zbruch" the narrator behaves like a Cossack among the Jews with whom he is quartered. To Gedali he speaks with the harsh justification of the activist: "She cannot help but shoot, Gedali, because she is the Revolution."

In "My First Goose" there is a double confrontation between Cossack and narrator, narrator and the weak. The story opens with a verbal duel between the narrator and that Cossack *par excellence* Savitski in which attitudes on both sides are revealed. Savitski challenges the narrator, "You're one of those pacifiers and spectacles on your nose to boot. What a nasty little object." But the narrator is helpless to defend himself, for he "envied the flower and iron of that youth." The narrator's general relationship with the Cossacks then is that they despise him and he envies them and longs to be accepted by them. It is the Cossacks who are in the position of judges and choosers. They quickly make their choice and refuse to admit the narrator into their circle. The narrator turns to the old woman in whose yard they are camped to get food. The old lady immediately sees that he is a kindred soul and appeals to his sympathy: " 'Comrade,' she said after a pause, 'this business makes me want to hang myself.' " Now the narrator is in the position of choice. Will he acknowledge his kinship with the victimized, *bespectacled* old lady? But what could be more damaging to his dream of acceptance by the Cossacks than this instant recognition by the weak that he is one of their own? " 'Christ!' I muttered angrily and pushed the old woman in the chest with my fist. 'I don't have to have explanations with you.' " The goose is the symbolic offering to the Cossacks that represents the narrator's willingness to accept their way of things as well as the trigger to the brutal act against the old woman that signifies his rejection of her.

The narrator is caught between two standards: the Cossack standard of violence and assertion with justice as its chief moral principle, and the ethical standard of Babel's creative man with compassion and reconciliation as the chief moral principles. He recognizes in his own makeup a double weakness. He has the Cossack sense of outraged justice without the corresponding ability to act. Though passive he cannot accept humiliation or refrain from despising weakness. The narrator's double weakness casts a shadow of guilt across *Red Cavalry.* At the end of "Crossing the Zbruch" the Jewish woman turns upon the narrator with her unanswerable question: " 'And now I should wish to know,' cried the woman with sudden and terrible force, 'I should wish to know where in the whole world you could find another father like my father.' " The narrator is forced to share the guilt for her father's death. In "Gedali" he assumes responsibility for justifying the destruction of the town to the old man in the name of the Revolution. Among the Cossacks on the other hand he must assume responsibility for defeat because of his peculiar cowardice, which causes him to ride into battle with an unloaded gun.

In the story "Squadron Commander Trunov" Babel explores the peculiar nature of the narrator's guilt. One of the Cossacks makes an unexpected charge against the narrator: "There's a devil in you, Liutov. Why did you cripple

Trunov this morning?" As it turns out, "cripple" is hardly
the appropriate word, since Liutov merely argued with
Trunov about Trunov's unauthorized murder of prisoners.
Surely this seems an ethical and even courageous act. But
there is a hidden reason for the narrator's guilt. Immediately
after this argument Trunov dies in hopeless but heroic combat with planes commanded by the American major, Faunt-
Le-Roi.[6] By his heroic act he saves the rest of the squadron,
including the narrator, from death. Only one other member
of the squadron, the thief Vosmiletov, goes to his support.
The narrator's guilt is due to his having passed moral judgment on men like Trunov and Vosmiletov without knowing
their real standards. The narrator's words early in the story
("Paul is dead and there is no one to judge him on earth,
least of all, I") take on new meaning. The narrator's guilt,
then, is due to his simply being what he is.

The narrator re-enacts his guilt in story after story, now
as *intelligent*, now as Jew. The emblems of his role are now
his spectacles, now his poor seat on a horse. The outward
aspects change while the inner core remains the same. So,
too, with the Cossacks and the saints. Babel presses outward
to enlarge the representatives of the type, to close the circle.
But the secret of the work lies finally not in the heroes, but
in the patterns by which they are rendered heroes.

[6] In his diary Babel takes note of an American pilot, Frank
Mosher, a member of the Kosciusko Squadron commanded by
Major Faunt-Le-Roi, whose plane was shot down by Red soldiers.
(*Literaturnoe nasledstvo*, vol. 74, p. 498.)

7. Red Cavalry: Art Renders Justice

"Your Holiness," lame Vitold, the fence for stolen goods and watchman at the cemetery, then replied to the vicar, "In what does the all-merciful God see truth, and who will tell the ignorant folk about it? Isn't there more truth in the pictures of Pan Apolek which satisfy our pride, than in your words, full of blame and aristocratic wrath?"

Thus in the fifth story of *Red Cavalry*, Babel makes his first statement of the theme of the work: art should "satisfy our pride." It is characteristic of Babel's elusiveness that he has withheld an explicit statement of theme until the fifth story in the cycle, allowing the earlier stories to strike with full, unmediated force upon the reader's sensibilities. But the fifth story, "Pan Apolek," opens with a direct statement to the reader:

The excellent and wise life of Pan Apolek went to my head like old wine. In Novograd-Volynsk, in that hastily shattered town among twisted ruins, fate threw at my feet a gospel hidden from the world. Surrounded by the naive radiance of haloes, I then gave my vow to follow the example of Pan Apolek. And the sweetness of the dreamer's wrath, the bitter disdain for the curs and swine of mankind, the flame of silent and intoxicating revenge, I sacrificed to my new vow.

The hagiographic style is arresting, but even more so is the sense of relief we experience in at last coming upon a straightforward statement of belief. From the beginning of *Red Cavalry* our senses and our minds have been assaulted by shocking episodes told in an elliptical style free of explanation. The stories present a glittering, portentous, but resisting surface to the reader. He feels that he has been dealt a blow with a powerful instrument, but he cannot yet determine to what purpose. "Pan Apolek" is a story about art, it is a story setting forth a particular view of humanity, and it opens with a resounding affirmation from the author-narrator that this is his view of art, his view of humanity. The door opens wider. Here is a good place to enter Babel's world.

In each of the stories of *Red Cavalry* the narrator appears in the guise appropriate to the situation: as Red armyman, as *intelligent*, as Jew, as the observing eye. In "Pan Apolek" he appears for the first time as "writer," as "author of the work." His statement of belief in his role as writer occurs three times in the story: in his "vow" that opens the story, in the description of Apolek's paintings, and in the parable of Christ and Deborah. The writer in his vow renounces "the sweetness of the dreamer's wrath, the bitter disdain for the curs and swine of mankind, the flame of silent and intoxicating revenge." The belief is restated from the affirmative side in the description of Apolek's paintings, which "have elevated [the common people] to sainthood in their lifetimes." Apolek's parable about Deborah and Christ sums up the views of man that inform his art. According to Apolek, Deborah could not lie with her husband on her wedding night because, being filled with fear, she was seized with hiccups and vomiting. She was shamed before her family and the guests, but Christ, "seeing the unusual anguish of the woman, who longed for her husband, yet feared him, put on the bridegroom's raiment and, full of compassion, was joined with Deborah, lying in her vomit." Apolek's parable indicates that true humanity demands not only the acceptance of man in those attributes that elevate him, but also in those attributes that we despise. The parable underlines the writer's vow to reject his "bitter disdain for the curs and swine of mankind," but seems to require something beyond mere indifference to curs and swine.

The story binds together in the central symbolic figure, Apolek, two views of man. The first of these is the Christian view, which finds its place in Apolek's gospel when purged of the "aristocratic wrath" that is opposed to the Christly principle that the meek shall inherit the earth. Apolek is the preacher and exemplar of this Christianity of the meek. He takes his name Apollinarius from the heretic who "established so close a connection of the Logos with human flesh, that all the divine attributes were transferred to the human nature and all the human attributes to the divine and the two merged in *one* nature in Christ."[1] The narrator tells us that "chance almost made of the gentle wanderer the founder of a new heresy." It is of the essence of Apolek's art that he elevates the common people to sainthood, not by painting idealized portraits of them, but by painting them exactly as they are. When he paints "the Jewish girl Elka, daughter of unknown parents and mother of many bastard children," as Mary Magdalene, he unveils the truth about the Magdalene's humanity, for she was, as the narrator puts it, "the fornicatress from Magdala." Apolek does this not from a cynical desire to lower the saint in our eyes, but to point out that the human is inseparable from the godly. In the parable of Christ and Deborah, the price that Christ pays for his act of charity is mortality. "Jesus stood apart. A deathly sweat broke out on his body and the bee of sorrow stung his heart. Unnoticed by anyone, he went out of the hall of the feast and went off into the desert, to the east from Judea where John the Baptist awaited him." Jesus could not have remained God had he evaded the act of compassion, but having put on the bridegroom's raiment he cannot evade his humanity. A godliness lacking in specifically human attributes would have been of no use to Deborah or to mankind.

The other tradition upon which Babel draws in the story is the classical humanist tradition. Apolek's view of man requires from Christianity the emphasis on the lowly, the

[1] William Smith and Henry Wace, eds., *A Dictionary of Christian Biography* (Little, Brown and Co., Boston, 1877), p. 134.

meek, the grotesque, that quality that Erich Auerbach designates by the Latin word *humilis* and that he interprets thus: "In the Christian context everyday things . . . lose their baseness and become compatible with the lofty style; and conversely, the highest mysteries of the faith may be set forth in the simple words of the lowly style which everyone can understand." [2] Apolek's art is far from the idealized statuary of Greece. But from the classical tradition he (and Babel) requires the emphasis on physicality. Apolek's name also suggests Apollo, patron of art, and when he and his blind companion Gottfried play and sing in the courtyard of Shmerel's inn, "it looked as though the organ had been brought from St. Indeghilda's Church to Shmerel's and as though all the muses had sat down in a row at the organ wearing varicolored quilted scarfs and hobnailed German boots." In this single image Babel weds the Christian and classical traditions with the mundane world of the present. As important as the spiritual message of Apolek's art is his acceptance of the body. When the innkeeper sets out to catch Apolek, who has paid his bill by presenting Shmerel's wife with her sketched portrait, he is converted from the way of wrath by the memory of "the rosy body of Apolek, streaming with water and the sun in his yard and the quiet hum of the accordion."

In Apolek's painting the truth of the body ever asserts itself:

[2] *Literary Language and Its Public in Late Latin Antiquity and in the Middle Ages,* Bollingen Series LXXIV (New York: Pantheon Books, 1965), p. 37.

The new church was full of the bleating of herds, of
the dusty gold of sunsets and of straw-colored cows'
udders. Oxen with threadbare hides plodded under the
yoke, dogs with rosy muzzles ran before the flocks and
fat infants rocked in cradles swung from the straight
trunks of palms. The cradle was surrounded by the
brown tatters of Franciscan monks. The crowd of
Wise Men was gashed by shining bald heads with
wrinkles blood-red as wounds.

Here Babel uses a favorite device, the startling transformation over the space of the period from plural noun ("fat
infants rocked in cradles") to singular noun ("The cradle
was surrounded"). The switch from plural to singular
points to the combination of specificity and generality
in Apolek's painting and in his view of man. Each man is
individual and unique, especially in the possession of his
body with its distinguishing characteristics, just as the things
of the world have distinguishing characteristics and thus
become particular like the intricately carved Chinese rosary
that one of the wise men fingers in the painting. But man
also participates in a larger spiritual identity that is shared
by all men, which is our humanity. So the infant Christ is
plural and singular, plural in his symbolic identification with
the innocence of infants, singular in his mortal existence.
Hence also the "substitution" of one individual for another
—Elka for Mary Magdalene, lame Yanek for the Apostle
Paul, the Novograd priest for one of the Wise Men. The
substitutions are made in such a way that the individual

quality of the person, both physical and spiritual, is preserved. Yanek, the convert, "a timid-looking lame man with a ragged black beard, a village apostate," painted by Apolek in his individuality, reveals the human individuality of the Apostle Paul, also a convert and an epileptic. Sometimes the association between the actual and the mythical subjects of the paintings is elusive. One is puzzled at first by the painting of John the Baptist:

> The long figure of John the Baptist descended straight upon me out of the blue depths of the niche. A black cloak hung solemnly on that implacable, disgustingly emaciated body. Drops of blood shone in the round clasps of the cloak. John's head had been cut off at a slant from the jagged neck. The head lay on a clay dish held tightly in the large yellow hands of a soldier. The dead man's face seemed familiar to me. A premonition of the secret touched me. The dead head which lay on the clay dish had been painted from that of Pan Romuald, the fugitive priest's assistant. From the grinning mouth looped the tiny body of a snake with glittering scales. Its tenderly rosy head, full of animation, powerfully set off the dark background of the cloak.

Pan Romuald, the priest's assistant, is described in another story, "The Church at Novograd," as "a eunuch with a giant's body and a nasal twang" and as a "faithless monk, with . . . plump hands and [a] soul gentle and pitiless as the soul of a cat." He turns out to be a spy and is shot by

139

the Reds. The conceit of the snake reveals Apolek's divination of Romuald's treacherous character, but whence the identity with John the Baptist? The key seems to lie in the "implacable" nature of John, so opposed to the compassionate humanity of the Christ of Apolek's parable. Romuald is the representative of the Church, indifferent to humanity, pitiless in his judgments. It is also significant that Romuald and John are "eunuchs" and thus deprived of their humanity at the deepest level, as the Christ of Apolek's parable is not. Romuald's external differences from John are stripped away to reveal his identity with the implacable life-denying core of the Baptist, which betrays the Christian doctrine of forgiveness. Christ and Apolek possess the gift of compassion. It is this gift that the author-narrator proclaims essential to a humanistic art.

But beyond the attitude to be proclaimed in art lies the fact of art itself. It is here that Apolek unites at the most literal level the physical world of the body with the world of the spirit. In Pan Apolek the power of sight consumes and remakes the world. The remarkable intensity of the power of seeing is set off all the more by the presence in the story of Apolek's "eternal friend" blind Gottfried, in whom the faculty of hearing is as intensely concentrated as the faculty of seeing in Apolek: "Old Gottfried is beating out the tune with his shaky fingers. The blind man sits motionless in the yellow, oily glow of the lamp. Bowing his bald head, he listens to the endless music of his blindness and the mumbling of Apolek, his eternal friend."

What might be the power of an art that combines the

vitality of physical presence with a redefined humanism? Babel answers in another story, "In St. Valentine's Church," whose narrator sees the church in two aspects: first, as an aesthetic object, then as a spiritual symbol. The movement from one view to the other constitutes the essential action of the story. The narrator's change of view subtly enlarges the connections between Babel's new humanism as expounded in "Pan Apolek" and the task of the artist.

The story opens with an anecdote about the priest of St. Valentine's, one Tuzinkiewicz, who, "disguising himself as a peasant woman, . . . fled from Berestechko before the entrance of [the Red] troops." The narrator discovers two facts about him, that he was a good priest, "beloved of the Jews," and that he was responsible for the restoration of the three-hundred-year-old cathedral. On the day the newly restored cathedral was dedicated, Tuzinkiewicz was honored by prelates of the Church "in silk cassocks" and by peasants, "who knelt before him and kissed his hands." The anecdote suggests the effect of the cathedral's physical presence on the spiritual life of the community.

Seeking respite from his duties at staff headquarters, the narrator goes to the window and looks out at the church, "powerful and white. It glowed in the cool sun like a porcelain tower. Midday lightning flashed in its glossy sides, whose convex lines lightly ran down from the cupola's ancient green. Rosy veins smoldered in the white stone of the foundation and at the tops were columns thin as tapers." Later the narrator says, "The church stood before us, dazzling as a stage set." He enjoys the visual feast it provides but refuses to take the church seriously as a house of the spirit. Thus the action of the old woman who comes in, crawls before him, and kisses his feet seems grotesque, disconnected as it is in his mind from any motive. He has heard the organ pealing forth from the church and at that very moment sees the old woman appear in the staff headquarters, but the two events are not tied together in any way for him. Throughout the story he suffers from the inability to make the connection between events and motive, until he has the flash of revelation that makes his experience whole.

The old woman has come to appeal to him to save the church from the vandalism of the Cossacks. This fact gradually dawns on him as the organ "grew quiet and then guffawed in bass notes." The scene is masterly, with swift cutting between the sound of the organ, the old woman's pleas, and the narrator's fear of ridicule. Nowhere in the paragraph is there so much as a word of explicit statement. We are told what the narrator hears (the organ), what he sees (the purblind old woman embracing his feet), and what he does (he glances at the other men in the staff and tries to drag the old woman from his feet). No words are exchanged, nor is the narrator's dawning understanding stated. Only his action in running to the church makes clear his comprehension of the situation.

As the narrator runs, he sees another of those scenes in which dissociated elements strike the senses with equal force: "The side doors [of the church] were open and the skulls of horses dangled on the graves of Polish officers."

As he enters the altar room, he comes upon yet another strange scene. The nurse Sasha is rummaging through vestments. Cossacks enter and, pushing her down on the piles of materials, pretend to rape her. "And only then, passing through the altar, we entered the church," the narrator tells us. Why "and only then"? The narrator does not tell us, for he does not yet know that this is but one of several acts of desecration he is to witness.

As he enters the sanctuary, he is struck again by the beauty of the church, "full of dancing sunbeams, airy columns, a kind of cool gaiety," and by the paintings of Apolek that adorn the interior. Two paragraphs are devoted to the paintings. The first describes what is seen; the second, Apolek's "point of view toward the mortal sufferings of man." The paintings, like the paintings of Novograd-Volynsk, insist upon man in his physical aspect. The infant Jesus appears with "his toes protruding [from the cradle], his body lacquered with the hot sweat of morning." The twelve apostles appear, "their faces so close-shaven as to be blue, their flaming cloaks thrust out by round bellies." "In that church saints went to their deaths picturesquely as Italian singers and the executioners' black beards gleamed like the beard of Holophernes." Throughout the church and the paintings the mood is gay, and this gaiety seems to render frivolous the sufferings depicted. After examining the paintings, the narrator makes a cool judgment: "At first I did not notice any traces of destruction in the church, or at least they seemed slight to me." His casual modification of his judgment comes from this observation: "Only St.

Valentine's shrine had been broken. Bits of decayed wadding lay strewn under it with the ridiculous bones of the saint, more like the bones of a hen than anything else." While the first traces of "destruction" strike him as laughable and negligible, he is even more inclined to dismiss the next "desecration."

> And Afonka Bida was still playing the organ. Afonka was drunk, wild and all hacked up. He had returned to us just the day before with the horse he had seized from the peasants. Afonka was stubbornly trying to pick out a march on the organ and someone was trying to persuade him to stop in a sleepy voice: "Drop it, Afonka, let's go eat." But the Cossack wouldn't drop it. They were many, the songs of Afonka. Every sound was a song, and each sound was torn from another. The song, its dense melody, lasted a second and gave way to another. I listened as I looked about me. The traces of destruction seemed slight to me.

The narrator's view of Afonka is framed by his two assertions that no damage has taken place. From his point of view the church is intact, since the church is for him an aesthetic object. The harmonious structure is unharmed, even enhanced from the aesthetic point of view, by the destruction of the shrine. Even less is Afonka's song, so sympathetically apprehended by the narrator as an outpouring of spirit, a desecration of the sanctuary. As the narrator quickly notes before the paragraph ends, "But Pan Ludomirski, the bellringer of St. Valentine's Church and the old woman's husband, did not agree." We are thus moved from the narrator's point of view, in which the church is seen as an object, to Pan Ludomirski's point of view, in which the church is seen as a sanctuary.

The gestures of Pan Ludomirski appear grotesque to the narrator, as once again he fails to make the connection between gesture and motive. The old man falls to the floor in a gesture that recalls the grotesque supplications of his wife before the narrator: "The bellringer fell to the blue-tiled floor and raised his head, his blue nose rising above him like a flag over a dead man." The compelling picture of Pan Ludomirski is broken by the unveiling of Apolek's painting of Christ:

> His blue nose trembled above him and in that moment the velvet curtain over the altar swayed, and trembling slid aside. In the depths of the uncovered niche, on a background of sky furrowed by clouds, ran a bearded figure in an orange Polish coat, barefooted with torn and bleeding mouth. A hoarse howl rent our hearing. The man in the orange coat was being pursued by hatred and overtaken by the chase. He thrust out a hand to ward off the impending blow. From the hand blood flowed in a purple stream. A Cossack boy standing next to me cried out and, lowering his head, turned to run, though there was nothing to run from. The figure in the niche was no one but Jesus Christ—the most unusual depiction of God I have seen in my life.

Babel blurs the boundary between painting and external reality. The howl of hatred of the painted crowd is "heard" by the people observing the painting, and the Cossack boy runs as if being pursued. The mysterious falling away of the curtain suggests the Biblical event of the rending of the veil in the temple. The revelation of the painting to the narrator is full of the suggestion of mystery, but the painting contains no more mystery than Apolek's daring in identifying Christ's suffering as a recognizably human suffering.

> Pan Ludomirski's savior was a curly-haired Jew with a ragged beard and low furrowed brow. His sunken cheeks were painted carmine; delicate red brows arched over eyes closed with pain. His mouth was torn like a horse's lip. His Polish coat was clasped with a precious belt and beneath the coat writhed porcelain feet, painted, bare, pierced by silver nails.

The Christ of Pan Apolek's painting is both aesthetic object and spiritual symbol. The painting arouses the narrator's aesthetic enthusiasm (as we understand from his description of it) and Pan Ludomirski's religious fervor. Infused by the religious power of the painting, Pan Ludomirski is moved to action.

> Pan Ludomirski stood in a green frock coat under the statue. He raised a withered hand over us and cursed us. The Cossacks gaped and hung their yellow forelocks. The thundering voice of St. Valentine's bellringer anathematized us in the purest Latin. Then he turned away, fell on his knees and clasped the savior's feet.

For the first time the grotesque action becomes ennobling: falling upon the knees is a sign not of weakness but of power. The mediation of the painting makes the sources of Pan Ludomirski's secret power accessible to the narrator. Aesthetic sensibility opens the door to spiritual awareness. His view is changed:

> Upon returning to staff headquarters, I wrote a report to the division commander about the outrage to the religious feelings of the population. The church was ordered closed and the offenders, being liable for disciplinary action, were brought before a court martial.

The story returns at the close to the official military tone with which it opened. (Compare "Our division occupied Berestechko yesterday evening. The staff headquarters were set up in the house of the priest Tuzinkiewicz.") The coldness of the communiqué ironically conveys the narrator's new sensitivity, for the offense he points to is not the physical destruction of the shrine but the outrage to the religious feelings of the population. Thus, feeling takes its place among the realities that justice has to take into account.

The question arises, what did the narrator see in the painting that led to this reversal? The style of the story is cryptic. Scenes of pure description alternate with short statements of opinion. No explanation of motive bridges the gap between fact and decision. The reader must ask himself, what in the nature of the facts justifies the narrator's decision? In the episode with Afonka Bida the narrator makes clear that he sees Afonka's "song" as no desecration but as an outpouring of spirit related to his earlier suffering, perhaps more appropriate to the sanctuary than empty ritual. He thus shows himself to be a man keenly aware of spiritual potential. Earlier he had understood that Pan Ludomirski's wife was outraged in her religious sensibilities, since he ran to the church to see what was happening there; yet his description expresses ridicule for those feelings. How does he come to take them seriously?

I would suggest that the answer lies in the nature of sacrilege as revealed by Apolek's painting: sacrilege is an outrage to humanity rather than to God. Apolek's picture of Christ suffering in the flesh conveys to the narrator the suffering of Pan Ludomirski in the spirit. The barrier between man and God is erased in Apolek's painting as God becomes flesh and man participates in the godly spirit. The spirit of outrage for suffering is one that the narrator can share with Pan Ludomirski. Religion is no longer a silly superstition for him but an embodiment of this sense of outrage.

Aesthetic sensibility is linked through the mediation of the painting to moral sensibility. Artistic creation as an outpouring of the spirit is a moral act. The narrator's moral intuition about the roots of suffering that feed Afonka's wild behavior leads to aesthetic awareness, the hearing of the "song." In turn, his aesthetic response to the painting extends his moral sensibility. In the final turn of the wheel, the simple man Pan Ludomirski responds through his consciousness of suffering to Apolek's painting.

If Afonka Bida's action is condemned by the same principles used to justify it, what is the distinguishing feature that leads the narrator to his decision? The cold tone of the closing lines and the failure to mention Afonka Bida specifically (that he was the culprit responsible for the breaking of the shrine is made clear in the story "Afonka Bida") suggest a withdrawal before the dilemma imposed by judgment, an attempt to repress the sympathy that the narrator cannot help feeling for Afonka's act. It is in the nature of justice that a choice must be made, and the narrator as judge does not hesitate to choose—on the first occasion in the story for Afonka, on the second, against him. The explanation, which we must once again try to determine from the "facts" as presented, would seem to be that Afonka in the expression of his own suffering fails to respect the general suffering. One might go further and say that the decision is based on the inferiority of Afonka's art, which is private and chaotic, expressing his suffering only and failing to symbolize the greater suffering. If art is an expression of the quality of spiritual life, then to make a moral judgment on this basis is not absurd.

The story takes its movement from three bravura grotesque scenes, the old woman grasping the unwilling feet of the narrator, Afonka Bida at the organ (Peter Quince at the clavier!), Pan Ludomirski on his knees before his God. The story is crowned by the sublime grotesquerie of Apolek's painting. These scenes cut through the fabric of the narrator's meditations on the beauties of the church. Because they cannot be made to fit into his conception, the conception is shattered. The narrator is forced toward a broader understanding. It is easiest for the narrator to enter sympathetically into Afonka's feelings and to grasp the "song" behind his wild outpourings of sound because he

149

knows the story of Afonka's suffering over the loss of his horse and his joy at the possession of a new horse. The sounds that are unintelligible to uninformed ears are for the narrator the melody of Afonka's self-expression, his own primitive art. The grotesque gestures of Pan Ludomirski and his wife remain opaque to the narrator until Apolek's art mediates between him and these incomprehensible people.

The revelation of the painting illuminates not only the central event of the story but even the most casual and peripheral aspects of the narrator's experience. The Polish officers' skulls on the graves glimpsed as he ran to the church take their place among the desecrations he has witnessed. Once grotesque as the hen bones of the saint, the skulls now become emblems of suffering. Now, too, it becomes clear why Tuzenkiewicz, who loved the church and was loved by his parishioners, abandoned both, seemingly so frivolously. The grotesque picture of the priest fleeing in the clothes of a peasant woman takes its dignity from its identity with the fleeing Christ of Apolek's painting. Each event of the story, easy for the narrator to dismiss individually because trivial or grotesque, becomes dignified in the symbolic act of desecration rendered by the painting.

The story suggests that what is grotesque becomes human and even sublime when traced to its source in the spirit. (I hesitate to use another word. No other word seems to have the breadth and dignity appropriate to the all-inclusive quality of human responsiveness examined by Babel.) The elevation of the grotesque makes accountable much that would otherwise be puzzling in the tone of Babel's work. It is clear in these parables about art that one should not take the presence of the grotesque in Babel's work as a sign of irony directed against the characters. On the contrary, the grotesque is accepted here and elsewhere as the revealing sign of the individually human quality, the divinely human.

8. Stories of Childhood and Coming of Age

Before *Red Cavalry* appeared as a book, Babel had embarked on a new project, a cycle to be called *The Story of My Dovecot*. Babel had intended to write a series of sketches or stories based on his childhood for a number of years, as is indicated by the story written during his student days, "Childhood: At Grandmother's." [1] In 1925 he turned from work on *Red Cavalry* (as we have seen, without completing his plan) to work on the new cycle.

It is customary to consider only four of Babel's stories as part of this cycle: "The Story of My Dovecot," "First Love," "In the Basement," and "Awakening." I would also include "Di Grasso," "Guy de Maupassant," and "The Road." These stories are united by their tone of presentation—a cool objective narration of his past by the older, wiser narrator—and by the theme of coming of age through attaining to knowledge. Each returns to questions first raised in "The Story of My Dovecot," and all may reason-

---

[1] The manuscript of this story is entitled "Detstvo. II. U babushki," according to the editors of *Izbrannoe*, 1966. This indicates that even in 1915, Babel conceived of a cycle of sketches.

ably be included in the cycle, at least for critical purposes. In this cycle, Babel adopts most directly the tone and form of autobiography. His model is the Turgenev of *First Love*, a debt he acknowledges in the title of one of the stories. Turgenev's narrator is a man of mature years looking back upon the events of his adolescence and recalling his initiation into the adult world through his first exposure to passion, violence, and death. The older narrator sees more now than he saw in his youth. He sees that he did not escape the effects of a too-early knowledge that has determined the course of his life. So too do Babel's stories reflect the youthful longing for knowledge and experience, while assessing the price paid for them.

It is difficult to know to what extent the stories are autobiographical in the usual sense of the word. Babel had this to say about them in a letter to his relatives abroad:

> Before my departure [from Moscow to the country] I asked Katia to send you and Zhenia each a copy of *Young Guard*. I make my debut there after several years of silence with a short excerpt from a book which will come out under the title *The Story of My Dovecot*. The subjects are taken from my childhood, but much is made up [*privrano*], of course, and much is changed. When this book is finished, it will be clear why I had to go through all that.[2]

2 Letter of Oct. 14, 1931, to his mother. Published in *Vozdushnie puti* [Aerial Ways], 3, New York, 1963. The story to which he refers is "The Awakening" ("Probuzhdenie"), published in *Molodaia gvardiia* [Young Guard], Sept. 1931. The problem of

It seems safe to assert that these stories are not autobiographical in the sense of giving us the accurate details of Babel's experience (no more autobiographical are the *Red Cavalry* stories), but that, like Turgenev's *First Love,* they form a part of the author's spiritual biography. They reveal the formation of the attitudes toward life and experience that inform Babel's work.

The first of the stories to be written, the programmatic story for the cycle, is "The Story of My Dovecot." Here, Babel shows the pressure of history and social circumstance upon the individual life. It is an art he seems to have learned from Pushkin rather than Tolstoy: to "place" the individual in his historical context in a few lines and to show historical forces operating in the individual so that the reader's interest in his destiny is in no way diminished. The opening paragraphs of the story move outward from the center of the child's experience to the larger world, from the personal desire ("As a child I very much wanted to have a dovecot") to the historical placing ("That was in 1904"), from the past event to the narrator's present ("That province doesn't exist any longer. Our town was incorporated into the Odessa region").

Each of the first three paragraphs follows the same prin-

---

separating fact from fiction in the stories is formidable. It is known that the Babel family was not affected by the pogrom in Nikolaev in 1905 and that thus the chief incidents of "The Story of My Dovecot" and "First Love" are fictional. (See Judith Stora-Sandor, *Isaac Babel', 1894–1941: L'homme et l'oeuvre.*) The picture of the conflicting temperaments of his parents seems to have a basis in fact.

ciple of development. The statement of the significant biographical fact ("I wanted a dovecot"; "I was only ten and I was afraid of examinations"; "I was good at learning") is followed by the drawing in of the surrounding circumstances that will determine the way the fact appears in the social context: that he wanted a dovecot in 1904 in Kherson province, that he was afraid of exams in a city where only two of forty Jewish aspirants would be admitted to the gymnasium, that he was gifted at learning in a situation where a man could buy his son's way into the gymnasium.

The story expands not only in the direction of the historical and social context but in the direction of the context of the family and the Jewish community. These tensions are encompassed in the boy's relationship with his father, centered in the father's generous promise to buy the longed-for doves, a promise hedged by his demands for outstanding performance in the admission examinations. This personal situation in the family extends to the situation in the Jewish community, for the child's admission to the school is a way of acquiring status for the family. When the grain dealer Khariton Efrussi buys his son's way into the gymnasium ahead of young Babel, who had earned the place, it is an indication of the father's failure, for had he succeeded in life he would have bought his son in.

The opening paragraphs of the story reveal the psychic violence inherent in the situation in the extremity of the boy's yearning and fear, in the harshness of the father's demands, in the extremity of the father's reaction to the thwarting of his desire. ("My father suffered a great deal then. The incident of the minus threw him into despair.")

155

The situation threatens to erupt into physical violence: "He wanted to beat up Efrussi or to pay two longshoremen to beat him up, but mother dissuaded him."

The story turns outward at this point, from the insular world of the family and the Jewish community to the larger world, which for the boy is the world of school. The critical moments in the child's life are the times of exam-taking, for everything rides on his success for him and his father. The examinations are moments of delirium. Of the first examination he says: "I fell into an eternal waking dream, into a child's long dream of despair. I went to the examination in that dream and nevertheless did better than the rest." As the child undergoes the examination the following year (after having memorized the three textbooks line for line), he falls again into the state of delirium: "The trustee's assistant asked me about Peter the Great. I experienced a feeling then of forgetfulness, a feeling of the nearness of the end, of the abyss, a dry abyss full of ecstasy and despair." Here as elsewhere in Babel's stories, the attempt at fuller definition as the story progresses leads to a paradox, the despair of the first examination becomes ecstasy and despair. The necessity for this paradox, which contains the essential wisdom of the story, will unfold before us as the story continues.

In the dreamlike atmosphere of the examination the child experiences his first moment of true knowledge and release:

I knew about Peter the Great by heart from Putsyko-vich's history and from Pushkin's poems. I poured out these poems, the faces suddenly whirled around in my sight and became mixed up like cards from a new pack. They reshuffled themselves on the retina of my eyes, and in these moments, trembling, drawing myself up, hurrying, I shouted Pushkin's verses with all my might. I shouted them at length. No one interrupted my insane mouthings. Through a crimson blindness, through the freedom that overcame me, I saw only the old, inclined face of Piatnitski with his silver-streaked beard.

The freedom the child experiences is the freedom of dream. He gives himself up totally to the imaginary world of his learning, and for the moment even the reality of the examination with its pressures slips away from him. The escape from reality into the world of the imagination is one of the poles of freedom. The first movement of the story, the "school" movement, reaches its climax here. The pattern is one of tension and release.

But before the movement ends, there are two preparatory developments of theme. The coercion by the father, the stress of the examinations, the freedom of performance have all been for the child flights from knowledge of his situation. He has lived in a special world. Now we are again reminded of the child's ambiguous relationship to the external world. As he waits outside the examining room for word of success or failure, he is stalked as prey by the Russian schoolboys. Sensing danger, he "wakes up" from his fatigue-induced reverie. He is saved by the kindly intervention of Piatnitski; thus his knowledge of the realities of the world in which he must live remains incomplete.

The other subject that remains to be introduced before we can turn to the story proper (we are still waiting for the story of the dovecot) is the family. It is introduced with the father's moment of success and release. Upon receiving the news of his son's success at the exams, he throws a peasant out of his shop and closes it down in celebration, then rushes off to buy a school cap for his son. Here emerge the differing views of the mother and father on how to cope with a hostile world. The father has sent out the child armed with the knowledge of three textbooks, and up to this point he has been proven right, for the child triumphs. But he triumphs in the special set of conditions that we call school, and it remains to be seen how his knowledge will serve him outside school. The father believes in aggressive action against the world, but he has little sense of its dangers: "All the men in our family were trusting toward people and quick to unthinking action." The Babel menfolk are an interesting breed, rebels, dreamers, madmen. They all have only a tenuous hold on reality, but their incipient madness leads them into lives of adventure like Uncle Lev (who kidnaped the daughter of a supply officer and fled with her to California, where he abandoned her and "died in a house of ill repute among Negroes and Malays") or into poetry like the inspired liar Shoyl.

Now the child is being educated into the Babel madness, and the symptoms of delirium are upon him. This leads to conflict with the mother, who takes a different view of the world. When the child returns with the news that he has passed the examinations, "my poor mother barely got me away from the insane fellow [the father]. Mother was pale in that moment. She was experiencing fate. By turns she petted me and thrust me away in disgust. . . . Mother was pale. She was experiencing fate through my eyes and she looked at me as upon a cripple with bitter compassion, for she alone knew how unfortunate our family was." The mother's clear-sighted view of the realities of their situation leads her to withdraw before the hostile world. She fears to buy a school cap too soon, for "God would punish us and people would laugh at us." She understands other aspects of their situation as well: "Like all Jews, I was short, thin and suffered from headaches from studying. My mother, who had never been blinded by her husband's pauper pride and his incomprehensible faith that our family would someday become the strongest and richest on earth, saw all this. She did not expect success for us." In spite of this truth, so clearly seen by the mother, the father persists in his imaginings, which reach their climax at the ball he gives to celebrate his son's "victory." The ball is a triumphant moment in the story, a celebration of the best features of the kind of Jewish community to which the family belongs. The family's friends are hearty commercial men, outgoing and gay. Among them is the learned Liberman, a pious man versed in the Torah. Nevertheless, the rejoicing, the boastful speeches, the whole "pauper's ball" are far out of proportion to the event that inspires them and are rendered by the author with light irony. The point is made that the Jews

159

conceive of their situation as a battle and that they go into this battle eagerly so long as they have the choice of weapons: "Thus in ancient times David, the King of Judea, conquered Goliath and in like manner I had been victorious over Goliath. Thus our people would by the strength of the mind defeat our enemies who surround us and thirsted for our blood."

In the first half of the story, Babel sets in opposition Jew and Russian, desire and coercion, the historical and the private, knowledge from books and knowledge of life, reality and illusion. The characters are defined by the ways in which they fit into or react to these categories. But the process of definition of the categories becomes increasingly complicated as they cross into one another and blur. The Jew Efrussi is more the enemy of the Babel father and son than the Russian teacher Karavaev, who wishes the boy well. Karavaev's physical characteristics are emphasized, and it is a clear portrait of the enemy. His blond ruddiness links him with the peasant looters of the latter half of the story. Yet he is capable of feeling joy "for me and for Pushkin" when the child declaims Pushkin's verses on Peter the Great. There are categories in the story that transcend race, and the first of these is art and the community of art. Thus we see a pressure at work in the story toward a proper alignment of values, a pressure to find the true categories that "work" by supplying reliable information about the world.

The lines are drawn up and the author turns now to "the

story of the dovecot." We have reached the moment when the boy and his family will cross the path of history. History appears, as it must always appear to the individual observer, as a series of ridiculous, meaningless incidents. But Babel here, as in the events of the Polish campaign, seeks to go deeper, to understand the meaning of history as it touches the child's life and the lives of his family in the form of incident. Thus once again at this key moment in the story the author reminds us of the date and of its significance: "The incident I am relating, that is my admission to the first class of the gymnasium, took place in the fall of 1905. Tsar Nicholas was then bestowing a constitution upon the Russian people. Orators in worn-out coats were clambering onto the high curbs next to the building of the City Duma and speaking to the people."

The Sunday of October 20, 1905, as Babel describes it, is filled with a series of startling and seemingly gratuitous events. The first of these seem high-spirited, even frivolous. "From early morning on October 20 the boys next door were flying a kite right across from the police station and our water carrier, pomaded and red-faced, had quit work and was walking about the streets. Then we saw the baker Kalistov's sons dragging a leather gym horse out into the street. They started to do gymnastics in the middle of the road."

In such frivolities is the experience of freedom expressed. Another ominous sign is the appearance of the local policeman in a fancy sash. "The policeman out of uniform frightened my mother more than anything." This is the mother's moment. Disaster is her milieu, as victory is the father's. Disaster confirms her sense of the nature of the world.

Disaster touches the Babel family in the form of the acts of violence that befall young Babel and Granduncle Shoyl. The two acts seem at first disparate in significance, for one leads to no physical injury while the other leads to death. Yet the boy learns the same lesson from both about the nature of reality and of his relationship to it. This lesson is nowhere explicitly stated, although it is suggested in a number of places. To understand it we must make explicit the links between the various acts of that Sunday, from baker Kalistov's vaulting sons to the mob's murder of Shoyl. Two threads are apparent in the events of the day: the continuing connection between man and things, and the expression of freedom through the release of desire.

Early in the story Babel alerts us to the special importance of a love of things: "No one in the world has a stronger feeling for new things than children. Children tremble from that smell like a dog on a rabbit's track and experience the madness which later, when we grow up, we call inspiration." The child and his mother are united in this love of new things, which draws them together in a special intimacy. The chief motive force in the story is the child's desire for the pigeons. This desire leads him through the series of acts that comprise his education, formal and informal. The Sunday of the story is presented as the occasion for the fulfillment of desire for the poor, who covet the things sold in the shops of the better-off (and Jewish) merchants. These desires might seem to us ignoble, but within the context of the story they cannot be so considered. The same inspiration felt by the mother and child burns in the face of the woman looter: "Along the street ran a woman with a flaming, beautiful face. She was holding a clutch of fezzes in one arm and a bolt of cloth in the other. In a happy, despairing voice she summoned her lost children." Her combination of joy and despair is the sign of that freedom which we have seen the child experiencing earlier in the story.

The second thread running through the events of the day is the desire to express desires, to engage in the free play of spirit, to be seen, to be taken cognizance of, to have one's day. The giving of a constitution means only one thing to the illiterate poor—freedom—and they interpret freedom in the light of their own necessities and desires. To them freedom is not political in content. It means doing what one wants to do, getting what one wants. Babel shows that liberation lies in this as much as in more "noble" forms of expression.

It remains to be shown what bearing these explanations have upon the central events of the day. Makarenko's brutal act in smashing the boy's pigeons against his face has tended to stun readers and to turn their attention away from the circumstances in which the act takes place. But in Babel's stories acts in themselves are opaque and can only be understood by reference to motivation. Thus one must look for motivation as well as examine the consequences of the act.

The explanation of Makarenko's act lies in the sequence

of events that take place between the time the boy accosts him and the time he turns on the child. The child has over-heard something at the bird market that he does not under-stand (a cryptic allusion to the death of Shoyl). He stops in the street to ask the crippled Makarenko, whom the chil-dren love and trust, about the news. But the old man is caught up in his own drama. He is absorbed in his wife's inventory of the goods they have picked up in the looting, and he experiences anguish at the thought of their inade-quacy. ("He turned his whole body away from his wife as though knowing in advance that her answer would be un-bearable.") His anguish is the opposite of that joyous free-dom experienced by the successful looters, the anguish of a man deprived of his moment of freedom, of expression, of his place in the sun: " 'Bonnets,' shouted Makarenko. He choked and sounded as though he were crying. 'It's clear, Katherine, that God has picked on me, that I have to answer for everyone. People are carrying off whole bolts of cloth, people are getting everything that's coming to them, and we've got bonnets.' " The rationale of the looting as seen by its perpetrators is set forth clearly here. They are getting their just due, what God himself has allotted them.

But beyond this, Makarenko is victimized in a way more fundamental to Babel's code of justice: he is not seen, his desires are not taken cognizance of. First, he wheels his chair after the lady with the fezzes, shouting, "Where did you get that striped stuff?" She ignores him and runs on. Immediately after her a horse-drawn cart rumbles through the square, but the peasant boy inside it also ignores Makarenko's entreaties. The scene is stunning: the old cripple in his chair wheeling wildly about the vast square, crying out in entreaty and rage. He repeats the key line that "explains" his act: "God has picked on me. . . . But after all, I'm a human being, too." Only at this point does he turn to the child. Seeing the child's puffed-out blouse, he assumes that he has stolen something and in his desperation determines to have it. The final crushing disappointment is to discover nothing of value. " 'Pigeons,' Makarenko said and the wheels of his chair squeaked as he rode up to me. 'Pigeons,' he repeated and struck me on the cheek. He dealt me a stunning blow with the hand that was holding the pigeon . . . and I fell on the ground in my new coat." The act seems horrendous—a man brutally striking a child. But even here there are two details that bring the two victims into more equitable relationship. The first of these is the sound of the wheelchair. The second is the new coat.

Chance has brought the child into the place where he becomes involved in the tragic denouement of another man's drama. Makarenko's drama ends with the blow he deals. It is the last act left to him, but the tragedy is that this act which would affirm his humanity exhausts it. The story turns away from him and to the child, for whom the blow is not an end but a beginning.

The blow is followed by a moment when the world severely contracts for the child. He lies on the ground:

The world was tiny and awful. A little stone was lying in front of my eyes, a stone chipped off like the face of

165

an old woman with a large jaw. A piece of string lay not far off and a bunch of feathers, still breathing. My world was tiny and awful. I closed my eyes so as not to see it and pressed myself to the ground that lay beneath me in soothing dumbness. This trampled earth in no way resembled our life, or waiting for exams in our life. Somewhere Woe rode across it on a great steed, but the noise of the hoofbeats grew weaker and died away, and silence, the bitter silence that sometimes overwhelms children in their grief, suddenly annihilated the boundary between my body and the earth that was moving nowhere.

The protecting illusion that the idea of school and study supplies the child is ironically called "our life." Now the boy's vision is focused on things in their barest essentials, and what he sees has no resemblance to that illusory "life."

But the moment when the world contracts is followed by the moment of expansion and release. The child, having broken through to reality for the first time, to the truth of his situation and to pain, now is freed by the truth and experiences joy:

The earth smelled of the raw depths of the tomb, of flowers. I smelled it and began to cry without the least fear. I was walking along an unknown street set on either side with white boxes. I was walking in a getup of bloody feathers alone in the middle of sidewalks swept clean as on Sunday and I was crying bitterly, fully and happily as I have not cried again in my whole life.

Babel expresses here an attitude honored in Russian literature from Pushkin to Chekhov: the life-affirming power
of recognizing necessity. What is the content of the
knowledge that the child comes to, more as an awareness
of the senses than as a clearly formulated idea?

The child hears of his race from an outsider for the
first time at the examinations, when the trustee's assistant
Piatnitski says, "What a people your Jews are. They've got
a devil in them." The words are delicately ironic, for in
the context they are complimentary, referring to the child's
performance at the examinations, but in substance they
echo the old reproach. The next time, he hears of his race
from an outsider as he lies on the ground. Makarenko's
wife, Katia, says, "We ought to wipe out their spawn. I
can't stand their spawn or their smelly menfolk." (But
compare this with the Babel mother's opinion: "She didn't
like vodka and couldn't understand how anyone could like
it. For that reason she considered all Russians insane and
couldn't understand how women could live with Russian
husbands.") The child can only be freed from the bonds
of his Jewishness (his father's fantasies, his mother's anxie-
ties) by having his Jewishness made explicit. At the moment when necessity intrudes most sharply, when the
severe contraction of the world takes place, the spirit as-
sents to freedom. In the careful tracing of the meaning
behind the child's sensations we see most clearly the advantage of Babel's form of narration, which conveys to
us the child's apprehension of the world, but informed by
the adult's understanding.

As the child returns home he sees everywhere those incongruous episodes that are the substance of the day's history:

> In a side street a young peasant in a vest was breaking up the doorframe in Khariton Efrussi's house. He was breaking it up with a wooden mallet, throwing his whole body into it. Sighing, he smiled all around the kind smile of drunkenness, sweat and spiritual strength. The whole street was filled by the crunch, crack and song of the flying chips of wood. The peasant was hitting the frame only to bend double, to sweat and to shout unusual words in an unknown, un-Russian language. He shouted these words and sang, his blue eyes lacerating from within, until a religious procession appeared in the street coming from the Duma.

Thus, inadvertently, is justice done to Khariton Efrussi. But more important, thus is shown the full moment of exaltation and freedom, the moment of the "song." The scene has the intensity of a pagan rite; indeed, it is a pagan rite as witnessed by our anthropologist, the child, who has come among this strange tribe and whose eye wonderingly records its customs. The religious overtones of the scene are developed in the next scene, in which the procession is described.

The procession is another of Babel's bravura grotesque scenes. It might well have been painted by Pan Apolek: "Old men with dyed beards were carrying portraits of the neatly combed tsar. Banners with graveyard saints fluttered over the procession. Enflamed old women rushed forward." The crowd is described as a grotesque procession of unfortunates, and again we are reminded that this is the protest of the poor. But the incongruous elements are offset by the fierce energy of the forward movement. This mob is perhaps the very one that Shoyl challenged and that caused his death.

What was the meaning of Shoyl's death? Shoyl's stories, his inspired lies, were about the Polish insurrection of 1863 and how he saw the soldiers of Nicholas the First shoot Count Goldewskij and the other Polish insurgents. Shoyl lives in his fantasies, in a world of aristocratic heroism and self-sacrifice far removed from the realities of his fish market. He is the quintessential representative of the Babel male character, having stretched the span between reality and fantasy to the farthest points. Shoyl's death is the moment of realization of his fantasies, when he becomes fully himself by acting out his illusion of heroism.

The caretaker Kuzma instructs the child in the meaning of Shoyl's death. It is significant that at the end of the story the child returns neither to his father nor to his mother, but to Kuzma. Kuzma, like the mother, accepts things as they are, but his acceptance is casual and without fear. It is he who keeps vigil over dead Shoyl and prepares his body for burial. He has respect for the body, but no false shame before it. Kuzma approaches the body with homely simplicity. ("Kuzma fussed over the dead man's feet. He tied the jaws and kept glancing over the body to

169

see what else he could do for the dead man. He fussed
around as though over a new suit of clothes and settled
down only after combing the dead man's beard.") In his
actions he instructs the child in the proper attitude toward
our physical, bodily weakness, toward our mortality.

One of the most striking things in the story is its treatment of the dead body of Shoyl. Babel does not spare the
reader's sensibilities. He renders the scene in all its gro-
tesqueness: "There were two perch stuck into grandfather: one in the fly of his pants, the other in his mouth,
and although grandfather was dead, one of the perch was
still alive and quivered." Kuzma mediates the gruesome
reality of the dead man, making the link between the grotesque body and the heroic act: " 'He cursed them all,'
he said, smiling and looked over the corpse with love. 'If
the Tartars had come at him, he would have sent them
packing, but it was the Russians with their women, Rooski
women.[3] It hurts Rooskies to forgive anyone. I know these
Rooskies.' "

Kuzma admires Shoyl because Shoyl has taken a stand.
As a simple man he appreciates the act of heroism without
fully comprehending the intricate chain of associations that
brought it about. He hints, too, at a complication in the
view taken of the incident, for what had the Russian
women to forgive in Shoyl? Was it not the offense he
committed by standing in their way at their hour? In any

[3] Kuzma uses the Ukrainian derogatory word for Russian:
katsap.

case, having presented the child to the reality of his situation as victim, but also to the possibilities for heroism in that situation, Kuzma takes the child to his father. The child is now prepared to enter the world of Babel males, armed with a knowledge that they have not previously possessed. And having set forth the true and hidden meaning that he has discovered by his feat of understanding in writing the story, the narrator gives us, as his last word, the word he has withheld from us throughout the story: "Together with Kuzma I went to the house of the tax inspector where my parents were hid, having fled from the pogrom."

I have unfolded the implications of the story at length to show its depth and richness. Though we have returned to the southern regions of the Odessa stories, we have come a long way in our journey to understanding. The style of the new cycle of stories is austere in comparison with the old, in fulfillment of the desire that Babel expressed to a friend in the middle of the years he was at work on the stories: "It is more difficult for me to work than before. There are different demands upon me and the desire arises to transfer into another 'class'—the class of calm, clear, perceptive and meaningful writing." [4]

The stories of childhood take their beauty from the intricate structure of understanding that unites their smallest details into a deeply resonant whole. The stories' sublime

---

[4] From a letter to I. L. Livshits in 1928. Quoted by L. Livshits, "Materialy k tvorcheskoi biografii I. Babelia," p. 133.

economy becomes a means of reaching out to encompass a larger area of human concern.[5]

As he continues through the cycle, Babel applies the general hard-won understanding to one episode after another, showing how now this, now that incident is illuminated by the larger vision of human destiny, how experience is drawn together, given meaning, and made whole by the application of the new understanding. The understanding of desire that illuminates violence in "The Story of My Dovecot" is used to reveal the nature of passion in "First Love," the nature of truth in "In the Basement," the nature of art in "Di Grasso." In each story the other elements remain, for violence, passion, truth, and art are inextricably linked for Babel.

The story "In the Basement" deals more directly than any other story by Babel with the complicated relationships between truth and fiction. The opening sentences come straight to the point: "I was an untruthful little boy. That was because of reading." The story is centered in

[5] Those who think of Babel primarily as a brilliant stylistic innovator will, of course, prefer the earlier works. A Czech critic, Jiři Franěk, in his eagerness to advance the cause of stylistic inventiveness, has gone so far as to see these later stories as a period of decline in Babel's career. ("Babel a avantgarda." *Československá rusistika*, 13, 1968.) While we can sympathize with Franěk's intentions, we would be doing an injustice to Babel did we not observe the superb artistry of these stories. Frank O'Connor, on the other hand, in his desire for clarity elevates precisely the stories that Franěk finds weak and disparages those that Franěk praises (*The Lonely Voice*, pp. 361–371). Babel commands more resources as a writer than either critic will acknowledge.

the child and in his growing awareness of the nature of truth, for, as he says, "What existed was more amazing than what I made up but at the age of twelve, I did not yet know how things were to be between me and truth in this world."

At first the child has no friends because he spends all his time reading; but when his classmates discover his remarkable imagination, he becomes popular. The head of the class, the rich boy Mark Borgman, takes him in hand and a new social life begins for the lonely child. This life leads him into the world and is the source of many fantasies, but in the long run it makes possible his turn from fiction to truth.

Among the people who surround him, the boy finds many instances of failure to distinguish truth from fiction. When he is invited to the rich Borgmans', his aunt Bobka takes this as the beginning of a brilliant career for her nephew. At the Borgmans' there is talk about Mark's father's becoming the Russian trade representative and taking the family to England. Not to be outdone, young Babel makes up suitably fantastic stories about his own relatives that cast a powerful spell over the earnest young Borgman.

The moment of truth arrives when young Borgman must be invited in his turn to the Babels'. The true nature of the Babel family is revealed in the drunken uncle Simon-Wolf and the half-mad grandfather. Aunt Bobka and the boy contrive to conceal the truth by sending the grandfather to the neighbors' and by giving Uncle Simon money for the tavern. As we suspect, the ruse does not work. Drunken Uncle Simon returns in the middle of Borgman's visit, bearing a great chest and antlers that he has been led into buying. A family fight ensues, he knocks Bobka down, and the mad grandfather comes dashing back to intervene. The wonderful mad scene is extremely funny, but Babel manages to preserve the note of pathos, to keep before us the boy's despair at Borgman's discovery of the truth.

After Borgman has fled, mumbling polite words of excuse, young Babel tries to drown himself in the water barrel in the basement. He is discovered and pulled out by his grandfather, who makes a succinct and unsentimental comment on the situation: "Grandson, I'm going to take castor oil so I'll have something to lay on your grave." The crisis resolves itself, as in "First Love," in the boy's hysteria, which reflects his shock at coming face to face with truth but which will leave him prepared to live in the real world.

That reality has its compensations is kept before us throughout the story. When the boy manages to send Uncle Simon away before Mark's visit, he thinks: "The son of the bank director would never find out that my story about the goodness and strength of my uncle was false. Speaking in all conscience, if we consider the heart, this story was true and not a lie, but at first glance at the dirty and loud Simon-Wolf this incomprehensible truth was not apparent." Babel opposes the truth beneath the appearance of things to the fictions that we use to disguise the truth. The role of imagination is not to disguise the truth with fiction but to grasp the essential truth beneath the misleading disguise.

"Awakening" is among the most popular of Babel's stories. It shares with that other popular story, "The Death of Dolgushov," a deceptive transparency that pleases the reader and gives him to understand that at last he knows what the story is about. In these stories Babel comes closest to the conventional surface of his subjects and presents them in their most palatable forms: killing as an act of mercy, repression as the rather comic and familiar story of the little boy who is forced to take violin lessons. To the extent that "Awakening" can be received as the conventional story it is unsatisfactory, for it conceals the anguished travail leading to understanding at the very time that it benefits from it for its point. In Babel's other stories, even in the other stories of the childhood cycle, the style preserves the tension of the creative act. We feel the cost involved not as clumsiness but as a peculiar brilliance and power that set the stories apart from other stories. In "Awakening" there is a relaxation of tension. No doubt this benign style comes from Babel's own sense of ease with the materials now that he has reached understanding through the writing of the earlier stories. Seen in the context of the cycle the story gains, for we see how we arrive at this tranquility and transcendence.

"Awakening" takes its place in the cycle by showing the boy's grasp of another facet of reality, the sensuous nature of the world. The story basks in the radiance of the

Southern landscape, resurrected for the first time since the Odessa stories. As in "In the Basement," the child's bookishness cuts him off from a direct, physical relationship to the world. The barrier that study creates between the boy and real life is symbolized in the hated violin lessons, another instrument of the father's ambitions. His father hopes that the son will be a prodigy, as so many other Odessa Jewish children have been, and thus bring glory to the family.

In his discussion of the story, Lionel Trilling calls attention to the ignorance of the natural world that was typical of the Jews of the eastern ghettos.[6] It is touching to find Babel writing in his diary of the Polish campaign, "I am learning the names of plants." Babel displaces this fact back into childhood and makes a good Russian the "teacher" who reveals this knowledge to the boy. Old Nikitich, the true master who will educate the boy to his vocation of writing, is opposed to the false master, the violin teacher. Nikitich reads the boy's first literary effort, a tragedy, and advises him to acquire a greater knowledge of the natural world. "A man who doesn't live in nature like a stone or an animal won't write two lasting lines in his whole life."

The moment inevitably comes when the father discovers that the boy has been shirking his violin lessons. His rage is appropriate to a man who has had his life's dream torn from him. The boy locks himself in the toilet, where he hears his father outside the door recounting, in an insanely

[6] Introduction to *The Collected Stories*, p. 24.

calm voice, a formula from his life of fantasy: " 'I am an officer,' my father said. 'I own an estate. I go hunting. The peasants pay me rent. I place my son in the cadet corps. I don't have to worry about my son.' " Aunt Bobka smuggles the boy out of the house to save him from his father's wrath. As the two fugitives advance along the street, the boy has an acute sense of the physical reality of the world. The story ends, "I thought of escape."

"Awakening" has a special significance in the cycle, for it reveals more clearly than any other story why the child "had to go through all that." The meaning of his ordeal lies in his future vocation. Babel gives here a portrait of the artist as a very young man. Each episode reveals the impact on the individual sensibility of a growing awareness of life's choices.

But the stories have a significance that extends beyond the illumination of the artist's destiny. The childhood cycle is the sternest test of the vision of the world to which Babel submits his materials. The child is by his very situation a natural victim, and when he is a Jew the possibilities for pathos seem limitless. Babel escapes the pathetic note by transforming the child's ordeal into a journey to understanding. Unlike *Red Cavalry*, where he presented the modes of the just life in dramatic juxtaposition, in the childhood stories we find a probing beneath the surface of each attitude to find what in it may be said to resemble its opposite. Thus the child and the father, though open enemies in their attempts to fulfill conflicting desires, are secret allies in their attitude toward the world. In the childhood stories Babel manages to see experience whole in a way that is wholly satisfying. The stories have the true note of understanding, and the interpretations do not seem provisional and imposed, as they often do in *Red Cavalry*. When he turns back upon his own experience the view of man invented in the Odessa stories and tested in the *Red Cavalry* stories, Babel finds the best and most convincing correspondence between incident and interpretation. These stories are the culmination of the search initiated with the invention of Benia Krik.

9. The Final Word and the Silence

The cycle of stories about childhood was the last of the major cycles that Babel was to publish in his lifetime. In the final decade of his life he turned to new projects, to the drama, to attempts to write a novel. Yet perhaps the most important work of this period is Babel's "reconsiderations." He wrote new stories for each of the three major cycles, and though in some cases these stories appear to be revisions of earlier unpublished works, they are of a piece in tone and attitude, indicating that revisions must have been extensive. The stories reopen the basic questions of the cycles of which they form a part. They share the new "calm, perceptive" quality of the childhood cycle.

A number of the stories continue directly the "autobiographical" mode of the childhood stories. The cycle now moves forward into young manhood, with the addition of "Di Grasso," "Guy de Maupassant," and "The Road." More surprising are the stories added to the earlier cycles, for example, "Froim Grach," revised in its final form in 1928, but published recently for the first time.

In "Froim Grach," Babel mourns the passing of his

legendary heroes.[1] The bandits cooperate with the Bol-
sheviks during the Civil War, but afterward they return
to their lawless ways and are exterminated by the Cheka.
The story ends with a dialogue between the head of the
Odessa Cheka, Simen, and one of his men, Borovoi, who is
saddened by the ruthless treatment of the old heroes:

> Borovoi listened, sitting in his corner. He sat alone,
> far from the others. Simen went up to him after the
> meeting and took his hand.
> "I know that you are angry with me," he said, "but
> we are the only authority, Sasha, we are the authority
> of the state. You've got to remember that."
> "I'm not angry," Borovoi answered and turned
> away. "You aren't a native of Odessa. You can't know
> that there's a whole history connected with this old
> man here."
> They sat down side by side, the head of the Cheka,
> who was twenty-three years old, with his subordinate.
> Simen held Borovoi's hand in his and pressed it.
> "Answer me like a Chekist," he said after a silence.
> "Answer me like a revolutionary—what use would
> that man be in the future to society?"
> "I don't know." Borovoi didn't move and stared
> straight ahead. "Very likely, no use."
> He pulled himself together and drove away his
> memories. Then, livening up, he began to tell the

---

[1] Russian text in *Vozdushnye puti*, 3, p. 29. English translation
in *The Lonely Years*, p. 10.

Chekists who had come from Moscow about the life of Froim Grach, about his adroitness, his elusiveness, about his contempt for other men, all those amazing stories that are now a thing of the past.[2]

Borovoi's nostalgia reminds us of Babel's love for the "poetry" of the past, which he mentions in the letter quoted earlier. But the implications are clear here as in the letter. Times have changed, and Borovoi must adjust himself to the change. In this case, the romanticism of the Revolution that called for heroes has given way to the necessity for building a state. The task requires a different kind of man. The story "explains" this, but it is permeated by nostalgia for the romantic attitudes that are no longer possible.

Babel began a reconsideration of the themes of *Red Cavalry*, too, in a story added to the 1932 edition. This story, "Argamak," is the final story in *Red Cavalry* as we read it today and it reopens all the questions that seem to be satisfactorily resolved in "The Rabbi's Son."

Nothing so exemplifies the uneasy and questioning approach of the author to his work as Babel's return to *Red Cavalry*, his attempt to write a more satisfactory answer. In "Argamak" the conflict involves not two but three men. We no longer have a simple duality of active and passive characteristics. In fact, the chief conflict of the story takes place between two men of action, and our narrator's suffering is only an incidental by-product of the larger con-

[2] *Vozdushnye puti*, p. 33.

flict. The new type introduced here is the locksmith Baulin.

> In his twenty-two years Baulin had never known any worry. This quality, characteristic of thousands of Baulins, became an important factor in the victory of the Revolution. Baulin was hard, a man of few words, stubborn. The path of his life had been laid down. He knew no doubts about the correctness of this path. Deprivation came easy to him. He knew how to sleep sitting up. He slept, grasping one hand in the other and woke up so that his passage from oblivion to wakefulness was unnoticeable.

Baulin is a representative of the proletariat. His trade of locksmith was in itself a symbolic craft in the literature of the Revolution (see Stockman in *The Quiet Don;* the brother Artem in *How the Steel Was Tempered*). His toughness and ability to suffer deprivation, as well as his certainty about his chosen path, separate him from our narrator. He is the first member of his class to appear in *Red Cavalry*, and we can suppose several reasons for Babel's writing a story that includes him. The simplest is that Babel wanted to justify his work in the eyes of those critics who had condemned it for not sufficiently showing the role of the working class in the Revolution. This motivation almost certainly played some part in Babel's decision to write this story. We might also suppose that the portrayal of Baulin has something to do with Babel's encounters during the 1920's with similar representatives of the new "proletarian" point of view. There were many such clear-eyed, tough types among the Moscow intelligentsia, particularly in the group around RAPP, the organization for proletarian writers. Babel's editor Furmanov, with whom he seems to have had a certain kind of friendship, was an example of this direct, straightforward kind of man, although Furmanov was in many ways more gentle and genteel than the commoner representative of the type. At any rate, Babel must have felt that this type was yet another form of his antithesis, another threat to his identity as an artist and a man. His apprehensiveness is clear in the story, where by far the greatest threat is posed by Baulin, although it is not precisely he who feuds with the narrator. The narrator says, "One could expect no mercy under Baulin's command." It is precisely this lack of human feeling that involves Baulin with the narrator.

Babel's Cossack, whatever his limitations, could never be accused of a lack of fire and passion. In this new "story of a horse" our narrator is caught between the passionate thirst for vengeance of the Cossack Tikhomolov, whose horse Baulin has turned over to the narrator, and Baulin's icy indifference, which enables him to play God without regard for human feeling. Babel shows a new mode of victimization, and both Cossack and narrator are helpless before it.

This "reconsideration" of the heroes of the past is even more striking in Babel's play *Sunset*. The chief figures of this play are Benia Krik and his father, Mendel, both familiar to us from the Odessa stories. Yet in the play Benia has undergone such a transformation that one wonders why Babel chose to associate him with his earlier hero. In the Odessa stories Benia is bathed in a glamorous radiance. In *Sunset* he is a sinister and shadowy figure, who craves bourgeois conventionality. He is still in conflict with his father Mendel, but now it is because Mendel's brutality and lawlessness prevent the family from assuming a respectable place in the Jewish community.

The true hero of *Sunset* is Mendel Krik. Babel glorifies the anarchic, anticonventional, romantic aspects of Mendel's character. Mendel is a brute. He kicks his old wife in the chest. Yet he is a man with a dream. As with Benia in the Odessa stories or the Cossacks in *Red Cavalry*, Mendel bears the armor of virtue, albeit a peculiar kind.

It is significant that Mendel, who preserves to some degree the colorfulness and power of protest of the earlier heroes, does not triumph. His defeat by his sons marks a turn from the heroic mode in Babel's work to what can justly be called tragedy. This turn has been signaled in the childhood stories by the concentration on the father-child victims. At the end of *Sunset*, old Mendel appears on the stage at the party which his sons give to celebrate the wedding of their sister Dvoira (the symbol of the triumph of respectability). He has been beaten up by his sons, who have taken over his business. *Sunset* belongs to the series of works in which the anarchic forces of the spirit are defeated.

In his next play, *Maria*, Babel does not deal with the victim in the tragic sense, the great man brought low, but turns to characters whose fates are wholly beyond their control. In *Maria*, Babel treats his characters for the first time chiefly as representatives of their classes. Hence, the fates of the individual characters are inseparable from those of their classes. The play is set in Petrograd in 1920. In a series of tableaux Babel shows the characters who are members of the aristocracy—Liudmilla, her father the general, the saintly cellist Golitsyn—going to their ruin. Their downfall is attributable to their own acts and characters, which in turn are rooted in the class to which they belong. Liudmilla, the chief female character, is the victim of her own innocence and naiveté. Her life in society has not fitted her for the role she chooses to play. In her desire to build a nest for herself and her family, she becomes involved with criminals and winds up in the Cheka, where she disappears from sight. The climax comes with the death of her father, the scholarly old general, which opens the way for the new class.

The thieves and bandits, who represent a second class in *Maria*, are much changed from the Odessa stories. The dealer Dymshits is Jewish, but this is almost the only link that remains. The new interpretation of the bandits is symbolized by their physical ugliness and deformity. They are treated as an ugly phenomenon that is temporary and will soon disappear.

The third set of characters significantly does not appear until the eighth and last scene of the play. They are workers, the new people who come to end the play on an optimistic note with the worker's pregnant wife, Elena, bearer of the new life, enthroned in the old nobility's apartment and admired by all the workers who come in to mop and wash windows.

It is clear that on this level the play represents a return to the pathos and enforced optimism of the early work. Yet at the same time, Babel has introduced a note of heroism in the character of Maria. She never appears on stage, but the other characters refer to her frequently, and her "voice" emerges in the reading of a letter that she sends to her family. She is fighting with the First Cavalry in Poland. Her remarkable qualities are commented upon by all the characters. One says: "Of all of us Masha is the real woman. She has strength, courage." Maria is the only character who is able to overcome the limitations of her aristocratic class and survive into the new era. Her romance with Akim, the commander of her division and a former blacksmith, is symbolic of the wedding of the old life to the new. Yet Babel's attitude toward Maria is somewhat ambiguous. Through her failure to intervene in the family difficulties, she is responsible to some degree for her father's death and her sister's disappearance.

We recall that in the letter found between the pages of Babel's diary he had expressed his hope of finding his place in the new life created by the Revolution as a singer of "that which goes deeper." *Maria* is a desperate attempt to give the special Babelian interpretation to the formulas that by the middle thirties were requisite in Soviet literature. Babel uses the formulas about the course of history and the inevitable triumph of the working class. He tries to interpret them according to his old standard of justice and individual fulfillment. But the only "heroic" character, Maria, significantly never appears on the stage, and the ending in which the workers take over is weak and forced.

It is Babel's misfortune as an artist that his belief in individual justice became increasingly difficult to reconcile with the reality of life in the Soviet Union. His later works preserve the optimism, the elevation of men to saints, which was one of his two rules for a successful work of art. But the other rule, the close and accurate depiction of reality, could no longer be followed. This lack of convincing detail considerably weakens *Maria* and brings Babel, through no fault of his own, back to the sentimentality of his early works.

No account of Babel's work would be complete without some reference to his "silence." Babel's silence—that is, his failure to publish—was a familiar topic of comment in Soviet literary circles in the 1930's. Babel was constantly trying to explain and justify himself to the community. He made his best-known comments on the subject at the First Congress of Soviet Writers in 1934, when he said that he was a master of the art of silence. His silence has usually been interpreted in the West as a result of direct oppression or as a protest in the manner of Pasternak. This second interpretation has been supported by Ervin Sinkó (a Yugoslav writer of Hungarian nationality), who shared Babel's house in 1936 during a trip to the Soviet Union and who kept a diary of his stay there. Sinkó reports that Babel refused to publish because he did not want to submit to the kind of "corrections" that would be required by publishers.[3]

There is no doubt that the increasing severity of the regime toward writers and the restrictions on the writer's freedom to deal with Soviet reality affected Babel's later work, in particular, his play *Maria*. We may suppose that the weakness of the play was apparent to Babel and that, as an artist who insisted upon the most exacting standards, he refused to make further concessions.

I suggest that this pressure from political sources was felt by Babel not only directly as a force that prevented him from publishing stories which dealt with reality in the way he wanted to, but also indirectly. The reality of Soviet life no longer presented Babel with material that could be interpreted according to his optimistic formulas about the triumph of justice for the individual. Thus, the pressure is manifested not only in his silence but in the quality of the work of the later years.

In addition to these political pressures we must suppose other explanations for the phenomenon of his silence. An important qualification that must be kept in mind is that his silence was never absolute. In the early 1930's he was still publishing stories from the childhood cycle as well as isolated stories on other subjects such as "Oil" and "Guy de Maupassant." His play *Maria* was published in 1935, and after that he published several stories, "Di Grasso," "The Kiss," and "Sulak" in 1937. In speaking of Babel's silence, the critics initially meant that he had not published

[3] Ervin Sinkó, *Roman eines Romans*, p. 346.

another work comparable in scope and importance to *Red Cavalry*. Neither of Babel's plays was well received, and hence they did not count in the totaling up. This is very clear in a comment made in 1927 by a critic who was well disposed toward Babel's work:

> At the present a new task stands before prose; the problem of the novel, of the psychology of the hero, of *byt*. . . . Babel turned out to be just on the border of a change in literature. It is not by accident that he ceased to write novellas and, as it were, went on leave for the last two years. If he were to write and publish a story in the manner of *Red Cavalry* now, we would consider it a part of his earlier style. Therefore, we can understand his searchings and his roundabout routes: work on scenarios, a play—but so far all this is a reworking of the old. What was written by Babel a year, a year and a half ago, has become literary history. Literature moves forward now by other routes.[4]

Stepanov accurately describes a change that did take place in Soviet literature in the late 1920's and early 1930's. During the first half of the decade the tendency in prose was toward fragmentary forms. Many of the things published, particularly those dealing with the Revolution and Civil War, take the shape of notebooks, memoirs, disconnected

[4] N. Stepanov, "Novella Babelia" [Babel's Novella], *Stat'i i materialy* [Articles and Materials], edited by B. V. Kazanski and Iu. N. Tynianov, p. 40.

observations. We need only think of one of the most popular books of the period, Furmanov's *Chapaev*, to find a good example of the approach to literature typical of this period. Form and plot tended to suffer. On the other hand, literature gained immediacy from drawing upon contemporary history. Babel's stories of the Civil War share this fragmentary character. Certain aspects of the memoir form are preserved in the stories, particularly in the dating of episodes. The *Red Cavalry* stories, however, are very different from other stories of the time in their emphasis on form and style. These stories mark the transformation into art of the raw material of experience. *Red Cavalry* is without doubt the outstanding achievement in prose of the first half of the decade. It is both representative of and exceptional among the prose works of those years.

If we look at the second half of the decade, we see a different tendency. The most significant work can only be the first books of Sholokhov's *The Quiet Don*. In general in these last years the movement was in the direction of the novel, of a work with unified plot and of large scope. It is significant that the first important Soviet novel was produced in these years and no less significant that it deals with the same subject matter as the more fragmentary works of the earlier years. *The Quiet Don* is a logical extension of the great theme that preoccupied the writers of a decade. It combines Stepanov's prerequisites for the new literature: the novel form, emphasis on the psychology of the hero, and careful attention to *byt*, the Cossack way of life.

Gorki saw creative danger for Babel in his extraordinary laconism as early as 1925: "His laconism is a double-edged quality; it can teach or kill Babel." [5] Babel seems to have had some sense of this problem when he turned away from the novella to the drama. His career is characterized by a continuing search for new means of expression and by an impatience with old forms already tried. We may suppose, then, that in the thirties, in addition to the problems of a nonartistic nature that beset him, he was also confronting an artistic crisis, was casting about for a more developed form of expression.

Rumors reach us of other works by Babel from the 1920's that were never published. One of these is a cycle, to have been entitled *Velikaia Krinitsa*, that dealt with collectivization and that was based on Babel's actual observations of a village in the Ukraine. One chapter from this book, "Gapa Guzhva," was published in *Novyi mir* in 1931.[6] Another has recently come to light and has been published in several places in the West.[7] Like the other story, it is named after its chief character, "Kolyvushka."

[5] *Literaturnoe nasledstvo*, vol. 70, p. 389.

[6] "Gapa Guzhva," dated Spring 1930, and subtitled "The First Chapter of *Velikaia Krinitsa*." *Novyi mir*, 1931, no. 10, pp. 17–20. In English translation in *The Lonely Years*, p. 30. In some instances the village is called Velikaia Staritsa.

[7] In Russian in *Vozdushnye puti*, p. 45. In English translation in *The Lonely Years*, p. 3.

Publication of another story, "Adrian Morinets," which seems to have belonged to this cycle, was announced in *Novyi mir*, but the story never appeared.

It is clear that Babel's plan for the book is to make a myth expressive of the upheaval of collectivization. His mythical characters, curiously, come from the opposition rather than from the "good" Soviet side. There is some attempt to make Osmolovski, the judge charged with enforcing collectivization, into a heroic character: "The judge, who had been nicknamed in the district 'Two-Hundred-and-Sixteen-Per-Cent,' removed his glasses and covered his sore eyes with the palms of his hands. He had earned the nickname when he had managed to obtain that figure in grain deliveries throughout the reluctant town of Voronkov. Secrets, songs, popular legends had evolved around Osmolovski's percentage." [8]

The character of Osmolovski is completely overshadowed, however, by the great figure that Babel creates in the story, Gapa Guzhva, "our widow who has led all our young men astray." Gapa is comparable in her strength and vitality to Liubka Cossack. The question that she puts to Osmolovski is startling: "Judge, what will happen to the whores [in the new society]?" Osmolovski's answer ("They'll gradually disappear") must be taken as a sad one, since it is a denial of the vitality she represents. At the same time Babel stubbornly maintains that this sacrifice will lead to a better order.

In the second story, the kulak Kolyvushka, who is "dis-

[8] *The Lonely Years*, p. 37.

possessed" by his neighbors, becomes a startling prophetic figure at the end of the story: "Kolyvushka was standing there with his shirt hanging out from under his waistcoat, and his head all white. The night had silvered his mop of gypsy hair; not a black hair was left." The villagers reject the omen: "You've come to torment us with that white head of yours. Only we won't be tormented, Ivan. We're fed up with being tormented nowadays." [9] But the last thing we see in the story is Kolyvushka's silver head looming in the distance as he leaves Velikaia Staritsa forever.

In these fragments from a cycle of collectivization, we see Babel attempting to reconcile the political necessity to present a positive picture of developments in society with his own artistic necessity to look deeper into human nature, to look beyond the ephemeral effects of human action on society to the universal implications of this action. According to the prescribed formula, collectivization must be shown to be historically inevitable and a good thing for the people. In "Kolyvushka," Babel tries to reinterpret this formula. When Kolyvushka appears, white-haired, in the village, one man, Adrian Morinets, appeals to the crowd, "Let him stay and work. . . . Will he take food out of anybody's mouth?" The hunchback Zhitniak responds, "Yes, out of mine," and goes to get a shotgun to kill Kolyvushka, who turns and leaves the village. Babel attempts here to make Kolyvushka's "offense" concrete and personal by showing his claim to the right to exist as a restriction on the rights of another man, Zhitniak. But

[9] *Ibid.*, pp. 8–9.

this solution is unconvincing, and we can well understand why Babel did not continue the cycle.

Another of Babel's projects was undertaken at Gorki's instigation. After sternly criticizing *Maria*, Gorki gave Babel a piece of advice: "It occurs to me that you, a man who has his own sense of humor, often verging on sarcasm, should try to write a comedy." [10] Babel apparently took this advice to heart, for we find in his letters, "I am writing a comedy for which I have great hopes" (Feb. 3, 1935).[11] At this time Babel was particularly excited about dramatic form. He mentioned his work a number of times in his letters:

> A strange change has come over me—I don't feel like writing in prose. I want to use only the dramatic form. (Feb. 24, 1935)

> I can no longer write prose. . . . The only form that attracts me now is drama. And so, for many months, I've been sitting over a play which I haven't been able to bring off, but now, only a couple of weeks ago, to my great joy I saw a flash of light and it looks as though I'll be able to finish it. (March 31, 1935) [12]

The manuscript of the play has not survived, and since Babel never mentions finishing it we may wonder if the flash of light was sufficient to illuminate the writing to its completion.

Babel's last unfinished project is the work of the years

[10] *Literaturnoe nasledstvo*, vol. 70, p. 44.
[11] *The Lonely Years*, p. 272.   [12] *Ibid.*, pp. 275 and 279.

before his arrest in 1939. His widow, Antonina Nikolaevna Pirozhkova, reports that he produced a great deal of work in the final years of his life that was confiscated at the time of his arrest and that has never been found. Among these works, according to Madame Pirozhkova, was a full-length novel about the rehabilitation of a bandit and his integration into the new society. In his letters of the last years Babel indicated that he was working on what he considered to be his major work. We can assume that this is the novel to which Madame Pirozhkova refers. In May 1936, he wrote: "I am working on my own stuff now and it would seem that, after all these years of painful deliberation and search, I have found my road and am writing with an ease such as I haven't known for a long time. I hope to have some real results by the fall. Am in a state of great inspiration." (May 27, 1936) [13]

Ehrenburg refers to these works in his memoirs:

> The manuscripts of Babel's unpublished works disappeared. S. T. Hecht's notes reminded me of an excellent story by Isaac Emmanuilovich, "At the Troitsa Monastery." Babel read it to me in the spring of 1938. That story destroyed many illusions. It was a bitter and wise story. Along with the manuscripts of the stories, chapters of the novel he had begun were also lost. His widow searched for them in vain.[14]

The most striking work of these last years to survive is the short story "The Kiss," published in *Red Virgin Soil*

[13] *Ibid.*, p. 306.
[14] Ehrenburg, *Novyi mir*, no. 9, 1961, p. 148.

in July 1937. "The Kiss" is important not only because it is a fine story, but also because it is the third alternative ending to *Red Cavalry*.[15] It is a companion piece to the story that opens *Red Cavalry*, "Crossing the Zbruch," and might well be titled "Crossing out of Poland."[16] It is a strange story indeed. The relationship between narrator and Cossack has altered. The Cossack friend Surovtsev plays the role of Mephistopheles, whispering suggestions in the ear of the narrator, who drifts in a will-less state, borne along by the current of Surovtsev's amorality. He seduces and abandons a good woman who has counted on his help. Yet the story ends on a note of joy in escape.

The cold, objective tone of "The Kiss" is frightening. Babel has managed to look with his steady gaze at the dark side of the heart, at the acquiescence in evil of the man who supposes himself to be moral. Now a reconciliation between opposing types is achieved by showing a

[15] Babel's Czech translator, Jan Zabrana, has recognized this fact and includes "Potselui" in the *Red Cavalry* cycle. Soviet editions follow a more conservative practice and publish it separately among other stories. It seems likely that Babel would have included it in *Red Cavalry*, as he included "Argamak," had he lived to see another edition of his work through the press.

[16] The title is probably borrowed from Chekhov's story about a cavalry officer who transforms a kiss that he had received in an incident of mistaken identity into the chief passion of his life. When he returns to the town where the episode took place, he is overcome by the recognition that he has invested his whole emotional life in a fantasy that can have no hope of realization. Babel's use of Chekhov's title is ironic, as is his use of Turgenev's title *First Love*. Both titles point to the differences between the stories as much as to likeness.

fundamental unity in evil rather than in good. One can but wonder what somber thoughts and experiences brought Babel to this deep cynicism, a seeming rejection of the belief in human goodness that he had maintained through the most devastating experiences.

What was the true course of Babel's career? How did he develop as a writer? Would the work of his last years have been another brilliant return to the spotlight? These are questions that can be answered only if and when the lost manuscripts are discovered. Until then it is best to avoid idle speculation and to turn to the treasure that Babel has left us.

10. The Short Story
as Contemplation

From the operatic Odessa stories, where we hear Babel exalting in the newly discovered powers of his voice, to the late stories with their hard-won effortlessness, we are aware of being in the presence of a stunning performer. The poet, says Robert Frost, is "a man of prowess, just like an athlete . . . a performer." [1] Yet Babel's virtuosity should not hide from us the searching seriousness of his stories.

Babel is remembered for his look of intense scrutiny. "Everything about Babel gave an impression of all-consuming curiosity—the way he held his head, his mouth and chin, and particularly his eyes," writes Nadezhda Mandelshtam. "It is not often that one sees such undisguised curiosity in the eyes of a grownup. I had the feeling that Babel's main driving force was the unbridled

[1] In an interview with Richard Poirier, *Interviews with Robert Frost*, edited by Edward Connery Lathem (New York: Holt, Rinehart and Winston, 1966), p. 232.

curosity with which he scrutinized life and people." [2] We feel this curiosity operating in the stories, where Babel is determined to examine everything and not to turn away from any human act. The same curiosity led him to join Budenny's First Cavalry in 1920 and to make friends with Yezhov and the Chekists at the height of the purges. The poet Mandelshtam asked why "he was so drawn to 'militia men': was it a desire to see what it was like in the exclusive store where the merchandise was death? Did he just want to touch it with his fingers?" Babel replied, "I don't want to touch it with my fingers—I just like to have a sniff and see what it smells like." [3]

It is the transfiguration by the mind's intense scrutiny at work upon the opaque materials of human action that produces the Babelian consciousness, that cool breath so familiar to the readers of his stories. Louis Martz has sought to describe "the poem of the mind, seeking to find what will suffice. It destroys the old romantic tenements, and in their place constructs a stage on which an insatiable actor presents to the mind the action of an inward search." The goal of the search for those modern writers who embarked on it was unity of being and the act of writing was not only the record of the search but its very process. As Martz writes, "Meditative poetry displays an actor who, first of all, seeks himself in himself; but not because he is self-centered in our sense of that term—no, he seeks him-

[2] *Hope Against Hope: A Memoir*, translated by Max Hayward (New York: Atheneum, 1970), p. 321.
[3] *Ibid.*, p. 321.

self in himself in order to discover or to construct a firm position from which he can include the universe." [4]

Babel is a product of the Russian avant-garde movement in literature that was so vigorous in the teens and early twenties of the century. He is a product of the Revolution, belonging to that group of writers emerging in the early twenties who made the Revolution their theme. Yet these facts finally become incidental to defining Babel's place as a writer, as his Jewish upbringing becomes incidental. All contribute to what Babel was to become, are the paths by which he came to be what he was, but none of them can encompass the writer who finally was. To consider Babel as a product of the Russian avant-garde or as a writer of the Revolution or as a Jewish writer is to diminish him. Babel's work assumes its rightful place, can be justly measured and understood only in the larger context of the European avant-garde. The superficial similarity of Babel's characters to the heroes of Pilniak, Vsevolod Ivanov, and other writers of the Russian Civil War invites comparison. But these writers are not contemplative and so the comparison flattens Babel's stories, makes them seem less than they are. For adequate comparisons, we must turn to a literature that displays a deeper sense of adequate form. [5]

[4] Louis L. Martz, *The Poem of the Mind* (New York: Oxford University Press, 1966), pp. 4 and 31. It is significant that to find an exact equivalent for Babel's place we must turn to studies of modern poetry.

[5] This is a flaw of Robert Maguire's useful and interesting study, *Red Virgin Soil*. When Maguire applies to Babel the insights that are yielded by an examination of his work in the con-

The clue to Babel's special qualities lies in that voice that never ceases to arrest our attention when we hear it. It has its own timbre, but it is akin to other voices that combine passion with meditation, extravagance with discipline—to John Donne's voice, say, or Wallace Stevens's. Characteristically, it is the quality of the voice that gives meditative literature a claim on our attention, that guarantees the authenticity of the act of the mind that it describes. Thus, no tone or language can be too extravagant, too rhetorical, or too decorative. Language is judged by its effectiveness in expressing the state of mind that it describes or, even beyond this, by its adequacy to the act of the mind which it imitates and of which it is a part. In Babel we see the voice displaying the anguish of its plight in verbal fireworks and finding the fireworks an adequate correspondence to the tension and ambiguity present in the mind's quest. But as the mind through its own action achieves greater control over the processes of contemplation, Babel strives for a more austere style that will be the instrument of control just as it is its reflection.

It is characteristic of this art that to succeed, it has to be tuned to a fine pitch. An effort that fails to sustain a perfectly conceived tension among the parts, which might

---

text of the work of other writers who published in *Red Virgin Soil*, Babel's work emerges flat and reduced. This is the inevitable result of the nature of the book, whose aim is to concentrate and focus the twenties for us. Babel appears at his worst when seen as part of "the twenties," at his best when his unique qualities are singled out.

be completely satisfying in a less rigorous kind of art, falls completely flat here. That Babel himself was well aware of this fact is clear from the rigorous criteria he exercised on his own work, continually excluding from the collected works those stories that failed to meet his high standard. Many of these rejected stories have been republished recently and have met with critical success. Any story by Babel can be read with interest, but Babel was surely right in thinking that these stories do not belong to that ideal body of work which he envisioned and toward which he strove.[6]

Babel's most profound tie with the great tradition of modern literature is in his recreating of his world.[7] Richard Ellmann writes that the modern artist is likely "to be defiantly aesthetic in his view of the mind, of 'ideas' and of knowledge itself."[8] In Babel the important ideas are those that can be conceived by the imagination, and they are presented to us clothed in the forms of the imagination. The stories are logical, often even rigorous, in their struc-

---

[6] It is unfortunate that the outlines of Babel's "ideal" work are obscured by other considerations. Often for political reasons he included in his collected works stories like "Karl-Yankel" and "Oil," which he regarded as poor.

[7] Richard Ellmann, in the introduction to *The Modern Tradition* (New York: Oxford University Press, 1955), writes of the symbolist (he uses the term in a broad sense), "He is explaining the possibility of a basic shift in emphasis—from physical to mental reality, from the multiplicity of sense experience to unifying ideas, from the objects of knowledge to the process of knowing" (p. 7).

[8] *Ibid.*

ture, but it is the special logic of the imagination that requires us to link together events and acts that initially seem unlike.

Malraux has observed, "The [modern] artist has not only expelled his masters from the canvas, but reality as well—not necessarily the outer aspects of reality, but reality at its deepest level—the 'scheme of things'—and replaced it by his own." [9] As Martz puts it, the work of art as meditation outlived the age of belief in which it had its beginnings and came to be a surrogate for those feelings and exercises, those submissions in which the religious man of an earlier age found a sense of wholeness.[10] In Babel's work we find the two combined, as Babel strives to re-create his world through contemplating the relationships that the mind can propose among the shattered fragments of reality.

A simple statement of the beliefs underlying Babel's works, the basic goodness of man, the saving power of art, seems inadequate to their enigmatic suggestiveness. The special effect of his work is of being placed outside time, of being caught in a single recurring event, of going from innocence to knowledge in a flash. He has an acute sense of the artist's making of the object as a way of acting in the world. What is valuable to us in his stories is not the conclusions that they offer but the process of an intense straining after truth that they both exemplify and communicate. If we are able to see Babel's stories in their rigor and formal beauty as perfectly realized acts of contempla-

[9] *Ibid.*, p. 518.   [10] Martz, p. 35.

tion, then we shall have a clearer appreciation of the nature of his achievement. That achievement can be shown almost graphically by tracing the distance that separates the genial, poignant sketches he produced when not submitting himself to his own artistic rigor from the hard, bright, and altogether original works he produced when under maximum imaginative stress.

The secret of the brilliance of Babel's story lies in his holding together, in a severely limited space, through a tour de force of style the historical moment and the individual wish. Babel's interest in history is concentrated on the single moment in the life of a man when history is suddenly felt as individual choice. His curiosity about this moment draws him near the surrealists, of whom Ferdinand Alquié writes: "[They] do not tell us clearly whether they approve or disapprove of the properly sadistic act. They make us partake by giving it a value, its troubling temptation; they make us live a totally pure revolt, revolt in the face of life, in the face of the very conditions of existence, before everything that constrains desire and love." [11] Yet in Babel's stories the act never stands alone. It is the object of contemplation. A consciousness plays over it, manifesting itself sometimes in nothing more than a compelling arrangement of the facts. The tension between the act of revolt and the play of consciousness produces the special Babelian irony, so difficult for the reader to comprehend.

[11] *The Philosophy of Surrealism* (Ann Arbor: University of Michigan Press, 1969), p. 52.

A Babel story is written against the ground of the expectations of Babel's "reader who is intelligent, well educated, with sensible and severe standards of taste." When the unexpected occurs, when the story begins to deviate from this reader's expectation, the deviation is experienced by the reader as irony. But the story continues beyond the point where the reader can comfortably assume that the author's expectations coincide with his own and that deviations are to be dismissed as irony. It is the method of Babel's art to intrude the unexpected, the deviant upon the reader to such a degree that he cannot comfortably rest in his expectations. Some commentators on Babel like Lionel Trilling and Frank O'Connor have chronicled their own discomfort and thereby entered more deeply into Babel's world than others. The experience of discomfort is the sign that Babel's irony is not that of the decent, educated man winking in complicity at his decent, educated reader. Babel has set himself a difficult task—to get beyond this easy complicity of reader and author. His entering wedge is inserted at the point where our romanticism leaves a gap, or makes an exception—where our defenses are down.

Babel's irony results from his strenuous attempt to close the gap between subject and reader, even between his heroes and himself. The sense of irony persists because we remain aware that the gap has not been quite closed, that as Maupassant says in his preface to *Pierre et Jean,*

Whatever be the genius of a weak, passionless man, loving solely science and work, he can never enter so

> completely into the body and soul of a robust, sensual,
> violent nature, stirred by every desire and even by
> every vice, as to comprehend and describe the secret
> impulses and sensations of such a different being, even
> though he may clearly foresee and narrate all the acts
> of his life. . . . The author can only describe him-
> self in describing his characters.[12]

And indeed it is not only between Babel's active men and
the author that the gap persists, but between the author
and the saintly men. A trace of irony lingers about the
depiction of Gedali and Apolek, for if the decent reader
and author are apt to accept the saintly men as models
closer to their expectations, they perhaps have not been
prepared to follow straight to the end all the implications
of such an acceptance. And again, it is here, in the surprising, uncomfortable implications of the situation, that
Babel finds his theme.

A determined curiosity can be a barrier as well as a
bridge. There is a sense of withdrawal in the stories and
in Babel's life, as though he understood that what he was
willing to contemplate might be too difficult for others.
Babel's friends report conversations that seem sentimental,
even maudlin, as though Babel was tapping some source
of feeling to compensate for that coolness, that withdrawal
of self and feeling, that mystery which they all registered.

Babel continually widens the range of what can be held

[12] Trans. by Adolph Cohn (New York: C. T. Brainard Publishing Co., 1910), p. 12.

together in the bounds of contemplation. In his fine late story "Guy de Maupassant" he extends his concern to finding the just relationship between our illusions and the truth of life about us. Thus we are led through a series of events and observations whose order is determined by, whose unity is found in, the act of contemplation. The story presents us with one character after another who lives in illusion: Kazantsev, whose world is Spain and the Quixote; Benderski, who is mad from the profits he has made on war supplies; Raissa, whose only passion is Maupassant. Babel's young narrator, the same mythologized image of himself as a young provincial storming Petersburg that figures in his autobiographical sketches, lives entirely in his illusions. He sees himself as a young Maupassant, sensual, touched by genius, invincible. Constant reminders of mortality appear before him, but he is oblivious to them.

The story reaches the climax of illusion as the narrator, presumably having seduced Raissa, leaves the Benderski house. The whole world becomes an extension of his fantasy, frightening but exhilarating. "I swayed from side to side, singing in a language I had just made up. In the tunnels of the streets, hung with chains of lights, the steamy fog billowed. Monsters roared behind the boiling walls. The roads amputated the legs of those walking on them." This is the moment of freedom celebrated by Babel in other stories, when the world is rendered fluid by the imagination and the spirit in its power takes up its song in an unknown tongue. But in this story Babel presses farther.

There remains a revelation beyond the revelation of freedom, and that is the revelation of necessity. The narrator comes, as at last he must come, back to his attic. There sits Kazantsev, plunged into sleep over his 1624 edition of *Don Quixote*, forever dead to the world. The narrator too picks up a book; but if books can be an escape from the world, they can also be a path by which we enter more fully into the truth of the world. Thus the narrator learns from Edouard Maynial's book on Maupassant the one thing he had not taken into account when choosing Maupassant as his guide in life:

> At twenty-five he experienced the first attack of congenital syphilis. The productivity and *joie de vivre* which were characteristic of him resisted the disease. At first he suffered from headaches and attacks of hypochondria. Then the specter of blindness rose before him. His vision weakened. He developed a suspicion of everyone, wanted to be alone, became quarrelsome. He struggled furiously, dashed around the Mediterranean in a yacht, fled to Tunis, Morocco, Central Africa. He continued writing constantly. Having attained fame, he cut his throat at the age of forty. He lost blood, but survived. He was locked up in a madhouse. There he crawled about on his hands and knees devouring his own excrement.[13] The last

[13] The phrase "devouring his own excrement" has been deleted from the 1957 and 1966 editions of Babel's work. It is found in the 1936 edition, the last prepared under Babel's supervision.

entry on his hospital report reads: "Monsieur de Maupassant va s'animaliser."

The author does not make a more explicit statement of the narrator's final discovery, but we see that he has at last been struck by the knowledge of mortality that he has successfully evaded throughout the story. He sees that Maupassant's creativity and passion was the source of his death. The animal in man can take two turns, giving life or bringing death. It is the knowledge of the connection between the two, that inexpressible "portent of truth," that moves forward out of the night and the fog to touch the narrator, thus bringing the author's meditation to its close.

The beauty of the story lies in the precision with which it distinguishes the elements of life and death at the very time that it shows that these cannot be finally distinguished. Summaries of three stories by Maupassant provide counterpoint, going from starkness to gaiety as the story takes an opposite course. The seven-page narrative seems expansive.

It is given a larger dimension by the implied lapse of time between the present of the narrator-author, who sits meditating upon the meaning of his experiences and drawing their spiritual design, and the past of the narrator-actor who plays the dual role of experiencer and the mind's pilgrim to knowledge. The space of the story enlarges, too, as the narrator's sense of the world balloons in the energy of his illusions. But finally the space and time of the story contract as the youthful narrator becomes one with the older narrator in the possession of knowledge. At the end of the story the narrator and we with him contract into the narrow space and time bounded by our mortality: "The fog came up to the window and hid the universe. My heart contracted. The portent of truth touched me."

Babel is put in touch with the truth through the emblematic life. When the superfluous is stripped away and the meaningful fragments are rearranged in their secret, true spiritual order, Babel finds what Geoffrey Hartman has called "the mediating presence." [14] In "Guy de Maupassant" the narrator cannot see the truth of his life until it is mediated to him by the emblematic life of Maupassant. Yet Babel's mediation is, in the final analysis, self-created. Its final authority rests in the authority of the artist who has made the design and proposed its interpretation. Thus, like the poets whom Hartman discusses, Babel is a part of that experiment "which clearing the mind for the shock of life, would in time overcome every arbitrary god of the intellect, thus to achieve a perfect induction and a faultless faith." [15]

[14] *The Unmediated Vision* (New York: Harcourt, Brace and World, Inc., 1966).
[15] *Ibid.*, p. 173.

Selected Bibliography

Russian-language material.

Annenkov, Yuri. *Dnevnik moikh vstrech*, vol. 1. New York: Inter-Language Literary Associates, 1966.

Babel, I. E. *Benia Krik. Kinopovest'*. Moscow: "Krug," 1926.

——. *Bluzhdaiushchie zvezdy. Kinostsenarii*. Moscow: "Kinopechat'," 1926.

——. "Chetyre novelly" ("Froim Grach," "Moi pervyi gonorar," "Kolyvushka," and "Na pole chesti"). *Vozdushnye puti. Almanakh*, vol. 3. New York: R. N. Grynberg, 1963.

——. "Dnevnik." *Novaia zhizn'* (March 3, 13, 16 and 18; May 3 and 6, 1918).

——. "Gapa Guzhva." *Novyi mir* 10 (1931): 17–20.

——. "Grishchuk." *Izvestiia odesskogo gubispolkoma* (Feb, 23, 1923).

——. "Il'ia Isaakovich i Margarita Prokof'evna." *Letopis'* 11 (1916): 32–37.

——. *Istoriia moei golubiatni*. Moscow-Leningrad: "Zemlia i fabrika," 1927.

——. *Izbrannoe*. Moscow: Goslitizdat, 1957.

——. *Izbrannoe*. Moscow: "Khudozhestvennaia literatura," 1966.

Selected Bibliography

——. "Iz pisem k druz'iam." Edited by L. Livshits. *Znamia* 8 (1964), 146–165.

——. *Konarmiia*. Moscow-Leningrad: Gos. izd., 1926

——. "Mama, Rimma i Alla." *Letopis'* 11 (1916): 37–44.

——. *Mariia. P'esa v vos'mi kartinakh.* Moscow: Goslitizdat, 1936.

——. "Moi listki: Publichnaia biblioteka. Deviat'. Odessa. Vdokhnovenie." Zhurnal zhurnalov (nos. 48, 49, 51, 1916; nos. 7 and 16, 1917).

——. "Na pole chesti." "Desertir." "Semeistvo papashi Marescot." "Kvaker." *Lava* (Odessa) 1 (1920): 10–13.

——. "Novye materialy" ("Detstvo. U babushki," "Ee den'," "Iz planov i nabroskov k *Konarmii*"). Notes by I. A. Smirin. *Iz tvorcheskogo naslediia sovetskikh pisatelei. Literaturnoe nasledstvo,* vol. 74. Moscow: "Nauka," 1965.

——. "O tvorcheskom puti pisatelia." *Nash sovremennik* 4 (1964): 96–100.

——. "Publichnaia biblioteka." "Deviat'." *Literaturnaia Rossiia* 11 (March 13, 1964).

——."Rannie ocherki Babelia. ('Publichnaia biblioteka,' 'Deviat' ')." *Novaia russkaia slova,* March 29, 1964.

——. *Rasskazy.* Moscow: Goslitizdat, 1936.

——. "Staraia ploshchad', 4." Edited and with an introduction by L. Livshits. *Iskusstvo kino* 5 (1963): 57–78.

——. "Staryi Shloime." *Ogni 6* (1913): 3–4.

——. "Sulak." *Molodoi kolkhoznik* 6 (1937): 14.

——. "V shchelochky." *Siluety* 12 (1923): 5.

——. "Vecher u imperatritsy." *Siluety* 1 (1922): 7.

——. "Vyderzhki iz pisem I. E. Babelia k materi i sestre." *Vozdushnye puti. Al'manakh,* vol. 3. New York: R. N. Grynberg, 1963.

Selected Bibliography

———. "Zabytie rasskazy." *Znamia* 8 (1964): 122–145.
———. *Zakat*. Moscow: "Krug," 1928.
Benni, Ia. "I. Babel'." *Pechat' i revoliutsiia* 3 (1924): 135–139.
Bondarin, Sergei. "Razgovor so sverstnikom." *Nash sovremennik* 5 (1962): 175–192.
Budenny, S. "Babizm Babelia iz *Krasnoi novi*." *Oktiabr'* 3 (1924): 196–197.
———. "Otkrytoe pis'mo M. Gor'komy." *Pravda* (Oct. 26, 1928).
Ehrenburg, Il'ia. *Liudi, gody, zhizn'*. Vols. 8 and 9 of *Sobranie sochinenii*. Moscow: "Khudozhestvennaia literatura," 1966.
Frolov, V. *Zhanry sovetskoi dramaturgii*. Moscow: Sovetskii pisatel', 1957.
Furmanov, D. "I. Babel' (Literaturnye zapiski D. Furmanova)." *Voprosy literatury* 5 (1957): 206.
Gekht, S. *V gostiakh u molodezhi*. Moscow: Sovetskii pisatel', 1960.
———. "V Moskve i Odesse." *Nash sovremennik* 4 (1959): 226–240.
Goffenshefer, V. *Mirovozzrenie i masterstvo*. Moscow: Goslitizdat, 1936.
Gorki, Maxim. "Otvet S. Budennomy." *Pravda* (Nov. 27, 1928).
"Gorki-Babel'. Perepiska." *Maksim Gorki i sovetskie pisateli. Neizdannaia perepiska. Literaturnoe nasledstvo*, vol. 70. Moscow: "Nauka," 1963.
Il'inski, I. "Pravovye motivy v tvorchestve Babelia." *Krasnaia nov'* 7 (1926): 231–240.
Isbakh, A. *Na literaturnykh barrikadakh*. Moscow: 1964.
Kanzansky, B. V., and Tynianov, Iu. N., eds. *I. Babel'. Stat'i i materialy*. Moscow-Leningrad: "Academia," 1928.

Selected Bibliography

Kogan, P. *Literatura velikogo desiatiletiia.* Moscow: "Moskovskii rabochii," 1927.

Kruchenykh, A. *Zaumnyi iazyk u Seifulinoi, Vs. Ivanova, Leonova, Babelia, I. Sel'vinskogo, A. Veselogo i dr.* Moscow: Vserossiiskii soiuz poetov, 1925.

Kuvanova, L. K. "Furmanov i Babel." *Iz tvorcheskogo naslediia sovetskikh pisatelei. Literaturnoe nasledstvo,* vol. 74. Moscow: "Nauka," 1965.

Lezhnev, A. *Literaturnye budni.* Moscow: "Federatsiia," 1929.

Literaturnaia Odessa dvadtsatykh godov (tezisy mezhvuzovskoi nauchnoi konferentsii, 1964). Odessa: Odesskii Gosudarstvennyi Universitet, 1964.

Livshits, L. "Materialy k tvorcheskoi biografii I. Babelia." *Voprosy literatury* 4 (1964): 110–135.

Mirskii, Kn. D. Sviatopolk-. Review of Babel's *Rasskazy.* *Sovremennye zapiski* 26 (1925): 486–488.

Mundblit, G. "Isaak Emmanuilovich Babel' (Iz vospominanii)." *Znamia* 8 (1964): 166–174.

Nikulin, L. "Gody nashei zhizni." *Moskva* 7 (1964): 182–187.

——. "Proshloe v pis'makh." *Literaturnaia gazeta* (May 14, 1964).

Paustovski, Konstantin. "Kniga skitanii." *Novyi mir* 10 (1963): 63–118.

——. "Neskol'ko slov o Babele: Memuary." *Nedelia* 11–17 (1966). Reprinted in *Novoe russkoe slovo,* Oct. 2, 1966.

——. *Povest' o zhizni,* vol. 2. Moscow: "Khudozhestvennaia literatura," 1962.

Pertsov. V. "Kakaia byla pogoda v epokhy grazhdanskoi voiny?" *Novyi LEF* 7 (1927), 36–45.

——. *Pisatel' i novaia deistvitel'nost'*. Moscow. Sovetskii pisatel', 1958.

Pil'skii, Petr. *Zatumanivshiitsia mir*. Riga: 1929.

Poliak, L. M. "Literatura dvadtsatykh godov (1921–1929)." In *Istoriia russkoi sovetskoi literatury*. Moscow: MGU, 1958.

Russkie sovetskie pisateli: prozaiki. Bibliograficheskii ukazatel', vol. 1, edited by N. Ia. Morachevski. Leningrad: Publichnaia biblioteka, 1959. Section on I. Babel (pp. 103–118) edited by V. M. Akimov. See this comprehensive bibliography of Russian-language materials for information about editions and first publications of Babel's works, as well as for a fuller bibliography of materials from the early period of criticism.

Rzhevskii, Leonid. "Babel'-stilist." *Vozdushnye puti. Almanakh*, vol. 3. New York: R. N. Grynberg, 1963.

Shklovski, V. "Babel. K vykhodu knig *Konarmiia, Istoriia moei golubiatni i drugikh*." *Nasha gazeta* (June 12, 1926).

——. "I. Babel'. (Kriticheskii romans)". *LEF* 2 (1924): 152–155.

——. "O liudiakh, kotorye idyt po odnoi i toi zhe doroge i ob etom ne znaiut. Konets barokko." *Literaturnaia gazeta* (July 17, 1932).

——. "O proshlom i nastoiashchem." *Znamia* 11 (1937): 278–288.

——. *Zhili-byli*. Moscow: 1964.

Slonim, Mark. *Portrety sovetskikh pisatelei*. Paris: 1933.

Smirin, I. A. "Na puti k Konarmii." In *Iz tvorcheskogo naslediia sovetskikh pisatelei. Literaturnoe nasledstvo*, vol. 74. Moscow: "Nauka," 1965.

Selected Bibliography

———. "Odesskie Rasskazy I. E. Babelia." In *Trudy kafedry russkoi i zarubezhnoi literatury* 3 (1961). Alma-Ata.

———. "U istokov voennoi temy v tvorchestve I. Babelia (I. Babel i Gaston Vidal)." *Russkaia literatura* 1 (1967): 203–204.

Sushkevich, B. "*Zakat* v MKhAT II." *Novyi zritel'* 8 (1928): 13.

Timofeev, L. I. "Vvedenie." In *Istoriia russkoi sovetskoi literatury*, vol. I. Moscow: ANSSSR, 1958.

Tregub, S. Untitled article. *Literaturnaia Rossiia* (March 13, 1964).

Vinogradov, Ivan. *Bor'ba za stil'*. Leningrad: "Khudozhestvennaia literatura," 1937.

Voronski, A. *Literaturnye portraity*, vol. 1. Moscow: "Federatsiia," 1928.

Materials in other languages. (Only translations of Babel's works into English have been included. Book reviews have not been included.)

Alexandrova, Vera. *A History of Soviet Literature.* Translated by Mirra Ginsburg. New York: Doubleday, 1963.

Babel, I. E. *Benia Krik; A Film-novel.* Translated by Ivor Montagu and S. S. Nolbandov. London: Collet's, 1935.

———. Benya Krik, the Gangster and Other Stories. Edited by Avrahm Yarmolinsky. New York: Schocken Books, 1948.

———. *The Collected Stories.* Edited and translated by Walter Morison. Introduction by Lionel Trilling. New York: Criterion Books, 1955.

———. *Isaac Babel: The Lonely Years, 1925–1939* (letters from Babel to his family and nine short stories). Translated by

Andrew R. MacAndrew and Max Hayward. Introduction by Nathalie Babel. New York: Farrar, Straus and Co., 1964.

——. "The Journey" (translation of "Doroga"). *Dissonant Voices in Soviet Literature*. Edited by Patricia Blake and Max Hayward. New York: Pantheon Books, 1962.

——. *Lyubka the Cossack and Other Stories*. Translated by Andrew R. MacAndrew. New York: Signet, 1963.

——. *Maria*, a play in eight scenes with a foreword by Andrew Field. Translated by Denis Caslon. *Tri-Quarterly* 5: 7–36.

——. *Marya*. Translated by Michael Glenny and H. Shukman. In *Three Soviet Plays*. Middlesex, England: Penguin Books, 1966.

——. "Sunset." Translated by Raymond Rosenthal and Mirra Ginsburg. *Noonday 3*. New York: Noonday Press, 1960.

——. *Red Cavalry*. Translated by Nadia Helstein. New York: A. A. Knopf, 1929.

——. *You Must Know Everything. Stories 1915–1937*. Edited by Nathalie Babel. Translated by Max Hayward. New York: Farrar, Straus and Giroux, 1969.

Brown, E. J. *Russian Literature since the Revolution*. New York: Collier Books, 1963.

Carden, Patricia. "Babel: Story and Play." *Russian Literature Triquarterly* 3 (1972): 399–412.

Choseed, Bernard F. "Jews in Soviet Literature." In *Through the Glass of Soviet Literature*. Edited by Ernest J. Simmons New York: Columbia University Press, 1953.

Drozda, Miroslav. *Babel, Leonov, Solženicyn*. Prague: 1966.

Falen, James. "A Note on the Fate of Isaak Babel." *Slavic and East European Journal* 4 (1967): 398–404.

Selected Bibliography

Franěk, Jiři. "Babel a avantgarda." *Československá rusistika* 13 (1968): 155–162.

Hyman, S. E. *The Promised End.* New York: World Publishing Co., 1963.

Lee, Alice. "Epiphany in Babel's *Red Cavalry.*" *Russian Literature Triquarterly* 3 (1972): 249–260.

Leiter, Louis H. "A Reading of Isaac Babel's 'Crossing into Poland.' " *Studies in Short Fiction* 2 (1966): 199–206.

Leyda, Jay. *Kino: A History of the Russian and Soviet Film.* London: George Allen and Unwin, 1960.

Maguire, Robert A. *Red Virgin Soil: Soviet Literature in the 1920's.* Princeton, New Jersey: Princeton University Press, 1968.

Mathewson, Rufus W., Jr. *The Positive Hero in Russian Literature.* New York: Columbia University Press, 1968.

Mierau, Fritz, editor. *Die Reiterarmee mit Dokumenten und Aufsätzen im Anhang.* Leipzig: Universal-Bibliothek, 1969.

Murphy, A. B. "The Style of Isaak Babel." *The Slavonic and East European Review* (London) 103 (1966): 361–380.

O'Connor, Frank. *The Lonely Voice.* New York: Bantam Classics, 1968.

Olsoufieva, Maria. Preface to *Racconti proibiti e lettere intime.* Milan: Feltrinelli, 1961.

Poggioli, Renato. "Isaak Babel in Retrospect." *The Phoenix and the Spider.* Cambridge: Harvard University Press, 1957.

Pollak, Seweryn. "'Isaak Babel, czyli patos sceptyczny." In *Wyprawy za trzy morza.* Warsaw: Czytelnik, 1962.

Rosenthal, Raymond. "The Fate of Isaak Babel." *Commentary* 2 (1947): 126–131.

Sinkó, Ervin. *Roman eines Romans.* Translated into German

by Edmund Trugly, Jr. Cologne: Verlag Wissenschaft und Politik, 1962.

Slonim, Marc. *Soviet Russian Literature: Writers and Problems.* New York: Oxford University Press, 1964.

Stora-Sandor, Judith. *Isaac Babel', 1894–1941: L'homme et l'oeuvre.* Paris: Klincksieck, 1968.

Struve, Gleb. *Soviet Russian Literature.* Norman, Oklahoma: c. 1951.

Terras, Victor. "Line and Color: The Structure of I. Babel's Short Stories in *Red Cavalry.*" *Studies in Short Fiction* 2 (1966): 141–156.

Trilling, Lionel. *Beyond Culture: Essays on Literature and Learning.* New York: Viking, 1965.

van der Eng, J. "La description poétique chez Babel." *Dutch Contributions to the Fifth International Congress of Slavicists.* The Hague: Mouton and Co., 1963.

Zavalishin, Vyacheslav. *Early Soviet Writers.* New York: Frederick A. Praeger, 1958.

Index

NAMES

Index

WORKS OF BABEL

The Art of Isaac Babel

Designed by R. E. Rosenbaum.
Composed by Vail-Ballou Press, Inc.,
in 11 point linotype Janson, 3 points leaded,
with display lines in monotype Deepdene.
Printed letterpress from type by Vail-Ballou Press
on Warren's No. 66 text, 60 pound basis,
with the Cornell University Press watermark.
Bound by Vail-Ballou Press
in Columbia book cloth
and stamped in All Purpose foil.

Library of Congress Cataloging in Publication Data

(For library cataloging purposes only)
Carden, Patricia.
  The art of Isaac Babel.

  Bibliography: p.
  1. Babel', Isaak Émmanuilovich, 1894–1941.
I. Title.
PG3476.B2Z6   891.7'3'42   72-2359
ISBN 0-8014-0720-6